W9-BCL-356

The Hat

Trends and Traditions

The Hat

Trends and Traditions

Madeleine Ginsburg

BARRON'S

All inquiries should be addressed to
Barron's Educational Series, Inc.
250 Wireless Boulevard
Hauppauge, New York 11788

Designed and edited by
Anness Law Ltd,
4a The Old Forge
7 Caledonian Road
London N1 9DX

Series Editor: Madeleine Ginsburg

The publishers would like to thank
Siggi Hats Ltd. for the Italian straw hat shown on the jacket front,
modeled by Elizabeth Bacon and photographed by Dan Wesker.

ISBN 0-8120-6198-5

Printed in Czechoslovakia

PICTURE ACKNOWLEDGMENTS

The author and publishers wish to acknowledge the following picture sources, and apologize for any omissions:

a=above, b=below, l=left, m=middle, r=right, t=top

[Names in parentheses indicate location of painting or work]
9a (British Museum, London), 10 (Johannesburg Art Gallery), 11t (Brera, Milan), 12a, 26, 361, 37, 38b, 40, 42br, 75t, 98 (Victoria and Albert Museum, London), 14, 27t (British Library), 20b (Bodleian Library), 21b (Helsinki National Museum), 24b, 60b (National Gallery, London), 25b (Bibliothèque Nationale, Paris), 331, 49tr (Belvoir Castle), 34 (Vienna Kunsthistorisches Museum), 36 (Raniers House), 371 (Gemaldegalerie, Berlin), 39r, 84r (National Portrait Gallery, London), 42tl, 42tr, 65t, 92tr, 82t (Tate Gallery, London), 67 (National Maritime Museum, London), 48a (Kress Collection, National Collection, Washington), 49b (Musée du Louvre, Paris), 53 (Bethnal Green Museum, London), 631 (Metropolitan Museum of Art, New York), 73tr (Palais Galliera), 77 (Private collection), 86b (Worthing Museum, England), 83 (Chicago Art Institute), 90 (Thyssen Bormemisza Collection); 109 (Kodak Museum); 113b (International Exhibition, San Francisco).

Cecil Beaton: 118tr; Victoria Brown: 149; Richard Burbridge: 152t; M.E. Burkett: 22; Camera Press, London: 150; Henry Clarke: 128tl; The Fotomas Index; Frederick Fox: 153; John Freeman & Co: 35tl; Stephen Jones: 145, 147; J.S.: 137, 140; Claude Montana: 142; Moretti: 134; JS: 137t; Press Photo: 136; David Shilling: 148; Graham Smith: 151t; Philip Somerville: 139, 144t; Topham Picture Source; Vivienne Westwood: 146; Kirsten Woodward: 145.

The author and publishers would also like to thank the following for supplying pictures, materials for photography and helping so generously:

Sir Hardy Amies; Bunka University Costume Museum, Tokyo; Fiona Clark; Dior; Cora Ginsburg; International Wool Secretariat; Kodak Museum; Ralph Lauren; Millinery Institute of New York; Rougemont House Costume Museum, Exeter; Press Photo; Sears, Roebuck; Stockport Museum, Stockport; Wardown Park Museum, Luton.

Contents

	Foreword	6
1	Introduction	8
2	Medieval times	17
3	The Sixteenth Century	31
4	The Seventeenth Century	44
5	The Eighteenth Century	55
6	The Early Nineteenth Century	72
7	The Later Nineteenth Century	90
8	The Twentieth Century	113
9	Conclusion	139
	Glossary	153
	Bibliography	157
	Index	158

Foreword

Today ladies and gentlemen do not wear hats: they wear motor cars. Thus a large part of Madeleine Ginsburg's book is about the past and she deals with her subject admirably.

It is appropriate that the beaver hat is here discussed in detail. It is hard to believe how universally this was worn by both men and women a century ago. Today, sensitive as we are to changes in fashion — our anxieties fed by the fashion press and style columns in newspapers — it is difficult to imagine the shock of the trappers and felt-makers when they realized that their goods were no longer wanted. It was a notable example — one of the many — of suppliers and manufacturers failing to keep abreast of fashion and, in this case, important investments were endangered. The beaver is represented in the Arms of New York City an indication of how important that animal was to the foundation of the great trading station at the mouth of the Hudson, whose waters brought the skins from Canada.

Since the early 1930s, there has been a steady decline in the wearing of all types of hats for men. When I first came to live in London, I wore a bowler and did not feel pompous; there were still silk hats around in the city. It is strange that such formal headgear should derive from the hunting field, as did a man's tailcoat — now often worn for formal evening or for weddings — which is essentially a riding coat lacking a horse.

Today men who are interested in being fashionable tend to wear overcoats that are noticeably long. This is an elegant gesture, as long garments bestow dignity. The long overcoat really requires a hat to counterbalance the length. A felt or, better still, a velour with a moderately wide brim is most appropriate. The look created is serious and purposeful, though with a hint of dandyism.

The English have always known how to wear hats, their standards set and habits formed in early adulthood at Eton and Harrow, and in the Brigade of Guards. At Ascot they appear in their toppers and at smaller race meetings in their bowlers and green- or brown-brimmed felts. All are tilted well over the nose.

Ladies' hats have never displayed either the variety or the quality of men's hats. There are, of course, leading figures in the field of ladies' millinery: Freddie Fox, Philip Somerville, Graham Smith, and Simone Mirman, all of whom have managed to retain high standards without the backing of an industry behind them. Paris has always had armies of ribbon suppliers, hood-makers, flower-makers, feather-curlers, and block-makers upon whom all milliners have depended. It is a great pleasure to record that Pierre Debard of Maison Michel, the most active supplier of milliners all over the world, is still flourishing in Paris. He is renowned for supplying wood blocks and making new shapes, the shape dictating the way in which felt hoods are blocked, and the whole basis of the fashion statement made by the particular hat. Claudine Debard, the clever wife of Pierre Debard, has graduated from producing wooden hat blocks to designing and making hats herself, and exemplifies the possibility of an important supplier of milliner's accessories becoming a milliner. This is an interesting reflection of the state of the millinery industry, with a large number of the workrooms and couture houses closing down. They now sell Debard hats, under the couturier's labels, off the peg and onto the head. This is a sure sign of the weakening of the importance of "les chapeaux."

One of the great makers of custom-made hats was the famous Madame Paulette of Paris. On several occasions when I saw her fitting customers, she caressed the felt around the skull to ensure a perfect fit and tilted the brim to the most flattering angle. This attention to detail is still observed by some hat-makers who serve their customers well, but sadly both dress-making and millinery are suffering from a lack of young workers in the craft.

Mrs. Ginsburg quite rightly mentions Otto Lucas. I knew, admired, and laughed with him many times. Before the war he came from Berlin and settled into the London scene as comfortably as his thick accent would allow. He had built up a very successful business in expensive ladies' hats, sold to stores all over the world, for which he bought the shapes from the famous Madame Paulette and from Maison Michel. His success is measured by his popularity in all the grandest shops in New York. New Yorkers were amazed by the taste, technique, and international style of these designs from London.

My work in the army took me to Brussels immediately after the liberation. The Belgians suffered terribly during the War, but in a way quite different from the hardships of austere England. So it was with surprise and delight that we found the shops full of French scents, silk scarves, and flowers. Above all I noticed the opulent hats. Jackets had a military cut with wide, padded shoulders: skirts were short for cycling; but they let themselves go with the hats. Felt was scarce but strips of silk and wool were twisted into high turbans which in turn were decked in flowers.

A good hat flatters a face and enhances prestige. It invites coquetry and an infinite variety of elegant poses; a twist of the head turns a brim from a halo into a shield. The swan song of the hat was undoubtedly the Ascot races in the first years of the reign of George V and Queen Mary. These were memorably restaged by Cecil Beaton in *My Fair Lady*, carefully reconstructed from photographs taken at the time.

The hair that supported the large hats of the period was quickly cut off during World War I to become "The Bob." This introduced the distinctive cloche hat, which I well remember. It was worn by literally all women under fifty, a popular version being in bright yellow felt with bands of black or navy blue ribbon. I think it can be said that this was the last time the hat insisted on completing the costume.

Freddie Fox commented wryly on the Fifties and Sixties as being bad years for milliners. The shift dresses of Courrèges and Quant were so cheeky that the sobriety of the hat was unthinkable. There was therefore speculation as to whether Mary Quant would wear a hat when she went to get her OBE from the Queen, and surprise when she did. From this point, however, hair in a variety of styles, from shining page-boy crops to back-combed "hillocks" really took over from hats. Today there are a number of very pretty hats being produced, but the great tendency is for these to be worn on top of shocks of hair. The long neck is still an essential for elegance when wearing a hat, and this is enhanced by having the hair brushed up to unveil the nape of the neck. It is rare that hair on the shoulders carries a hat well. Madeleine Ginsburg's book gives a fine picture of the past and present of the hat and I hope it will also be an encouragement to the future.

SIR HARDY AMIES

Introduction

When the slogan "if you want to get ahead get a hat" was sent winging through the media in the 1950s by the British Felt Hat Manufacturer's Federation, it identified yearnings so basic to the human psyche, that they were common to humankind everywhere through time and throughout the world. The message was punchy and aggressive, promising men status and success, just for the price of the right hat. There was also a message here for women. Lilly Daché, queen of New York milliners, whose qualification, stated with charming certainty in her autobiography, *Talking Through My Hats* (1946), is "perhaps I have made more hats than any other woman in the world," rephrased it: "You see, a woman's hat is close to her heart, though she wears it on her head. It is her way of saying to the world: 'See this is what I am like' – or 'This is what I would like to be' ".

Worldwide industries have owed their prosperity to this concept. The crafts associated with hat-making and millinery are among the oldest listed in the guild and craft records, and the most widely used materials, felt and straw, are early and basic in covering and adornment. Social historians and anthropologists are in perennial debate on the motivation of clothing, and fashion as its dynamic; weighing up protection against status against sex appeal. The only constant is the inconsistency and the debate continues with a different answer for every generation. Ethnographers recording regional dress often find head coverings differentiated to provide a subtle yet precise social label for the wearer. But whichever area is studied, and whoever is assessed, head covering in some form

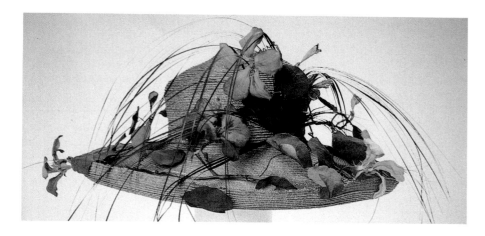

Right: A delightful confection of flowers, leaves and feathers on a timeless straw hat.

Below: William Tell refuses to bow to the Archduke's hat; a 19th-century engraving.

and for some circumstances seems a constant. The head, the seat of intelligence, needs extra protection and the proximity of head to face reinforces the effect of the expression and the personality. It can transform, the aim of Lilly Daché and her forebears and successors, or depersonalize, the ambition of every military outfitter. The effect can be very powerful. J.C. Fluegel in *The Psychology of Clothes* (1930), considers the removal of the hat as the removal of a trophy and symbolic of castration.

Its importance is reflected in the phrases in all languages which figuratively refer to the hat and indeed the hat alone was sometimes considered a substitute for authority. William Tell, hero of Swiss independence, legend has it, was provoked into revolt against Austrian domination of his native land, by the sight of the Duke of Austria's hat set on a pole in Altdorf as an object of reverence for the liberty-loving peasantry of Switzerland. The wicked Bailiff Gessler's revenge, for his refusal of homage to a mere hat, was, as every child knows, to order him to shoot an apple from his son's head – an unsuccessful attempt at poetic revenge. Fortunately both father and son lived to fight another day, and the Austrian domination was overthrown.

In the context of religious ritual, covering or baring the head, confirming or denying the personality, assumes great importance since it is bound up with different concepts of respect to a supreme being or overlord, as well as to family and society. The assumption is worldwide. A.C. Petitpierre in *The Hat* (Ciba Review, No 40), noted that the inhabitants of Tonga never covered their heads out of reverence for a god who was everywhere. In conventionally traditional Christian society, women cover their heads upon entering a church, the house of the Lord, and men bare theirs. The custom is central in the development of headgear in Western culture in its Judeo–Christian aspect, and derives from I Corinthians, Chapter 11. St. Paul's instructions, as given in the St. James version, the imperative for generations of hat wearers, state:

> But I would have you know that the head of every-man is Christ; and the head of the woman is the man; and the head of Christ is God. Every-man praying or prophesying having his head covered dishonoureth his head . . . For a man indeed ought not to cover his head, for as much as he is the image and glory of God.

For women, on the other hand:

> But every-woman that prayest or prophesieth with her head uncovered dishonoureth her head: for that is even all one as if she were shaven. For if the woman be not covered, let her also be shorn; but if it be a shame for a woman to be shorn or shaven, let her be covered . . . Neither was the man created for the woman; but the woman for the man. For this cause, ought the woman to have power on her head because of the angels . . . Judge in yourselves: is it comely that a woman pray unto God uncovered? Doth not even nature itself

Right: *Carrying the Law in the Synagogue,* a *c*1930 painting by W. Rothenstein, shows the men wearing caps and covering their heads with prayer shawls.

teach you, that if a man have long hair, it is a shame unto him? But if a woman have long hair, it is a glory to her: for her hair is given her as a covering.

There is much discussion about St. Paul's attitude which, "taken as gospel" or law, was a reflection of the realities of the life around him, the customs of the societies and cultures in which he moved. The clothes attitudes of Jewish societies have been described by Alfred Rubens in *A History of Jewish Costume* (1967), who saw covering the head now and in the past as a mixture of law and tradition. The practice then seems to have been that the priest covered his head when praising the Lord in the Temple, and that married women did not go bareheaded.

In biblical times, there was no obligation that a Jew cover his head at all times; now custom, in some cases observed as though it were law, arises from the instructions in the *Shulkan Aruch*, a compilation of ritual of the 12th century. Rubens suggests that it was a response to external pressures, requiring Jews to differentiate themselves by clothing or badge, from the societies in which they lived, which coincided with their own belief, Hukkath Hagoyim, that "the Jew should not copy alien ways." Within his lifetime Rubens observed changes taking place and that a headcovering for men "has developed into a moral obligation." This is now confirmed as a way of demonstrating Israeli nationality as well as a religious identity.

A similar combination of law and custom affects current Muslim practice. According to the *Concise Encyclopedia of Islam* (1989) ed. Cyril Glassé: "It is abominable to say the prayers with the head uncovered." Equally powerful is social custom, for: "Amongst Mohammedans it is considered a sign of disrespect to receive visitors with head uncovered. Consequently, at the approach of a

Above: Turkish men and women in the Piazza San Marco in Venice, the men wearing turbans and the women veiled. The Venetians are wearing simple black caps. From a late 15th-century painting by G. Bellini.

Above: Hat honor and etiquette: a gentleman bows and bares his head to a lady in this engraving by R. de Hoogh from *Figures à la Mode, c*1655.

visitor, the turban or cap is immediately placed on the head."

So profound and universal a concept extends into etiquette, manners and customs. In the 17th century, Christian convention, "hat honor" as it was called, required that a man bare his head in the presence of his moral or social superior; this was of profound social importance. In the summer of 1666, Samuel Pepys, socially insecure, ambitious government servant, worried, was to confide his concern to his diary, whether the Duke of York, brother of King Charles II, and as Lord High Admiral his civil service chief, considered that he had bared his head for long enough, even though he was not quite sure that he had been noticed at all . . .

But sometimes the social dimension had religious overtones and international implications. The Quakers, with their profound belief that all men were equal under the Lord, did not give "hat honor." George Fox, their founder, set down in his *Journals* during the 1650s: "When the Lord sent me forth in the world . . . he forbade me to put off my hat to any, high or low . . . neither might I bow . . ." Such principles marked an important stage in the life of William Penn, who was to be the founder of Pennsylvania. 24 years old, idealistic, a half-convinced Quaker, but still fashionably dressed, he returned home from the wars in 1664, but stood firm against the instructions of his father Admiral Sir William Penn, that he would accord "hat honor" either to his father, or to the King or the Duke of York. He lost three smart hats which his father snatched off in his wrath, and unable to compromise, left home. A convinced and conforming Quaker, he with his companions went to jail for refusing "hat honor" to the magistrate when arraigned in court. When ultimately he was to draft the constitution for Pennsylvania, he stressed non-denominational peaceful equality: a principle occasioned, if not caused by the loss of three smart hats.

The hat as status symbol was important from ancient times. In ancient Greece and Rome, a hat was the right of the free citizen but not of slaves. In being given his freedom, a slave was formally given a hat *capere pileum*. The red Phrygian cap was to reappear at the end of the 18th century as a symbol of liberty from oppression.

At the other end of the social scale, in the coronation ceremony, the exchanges of crown or diadem mark stages in regal authority. In the English coronation

Right: A Quaker meeting engraved by B. Picard for *Les Cérémonies Religieuses du Monde . . .* 1749. In accordance with Quaker practice, both men and women wear head coverings, the women having hoods and men broad-brimmed felt hats, conventional for class and period, but soon to become "fossilized" as Quaker "plain dress." The non-Quaker men have taken off their hats.

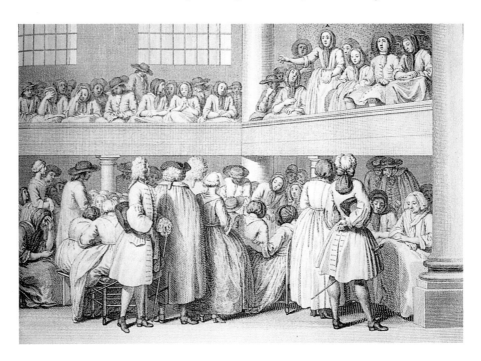

ritual for instance, there are three stages: the monarch processes to the altar with the crimson Cap of Maintenance, which is worn by both monarch and the nobility. At the moment of coronation, the crown of St. Edmund, the traditional crown of England, elements of which are said to go back to the days of King Alfred, is assumed; for the final procession from the Abbey of Westminster, this is replaced with the Imperial State crown. There are parallel graduations in church ceremonies, and the symbolism attached to the pope's crown and a bishop's miter is varied and complex. Their historical development from the simple caps of early Christian days precedes rather than explains the symbolism, and can be studied in works on church vestments.

An important attribute of the hat is its use as a badge of group identity. Flat caps were worn by 16th-century artisans and tradespeople, clothcaps by the same people in the 1920s and 1930s. Soldiers and police similarly advertise group identity and authority with theirs. Even before the introduction of full, regularized and stereotyped uniform in the 17th century, hats and caps in different forms were associated with groups of different convictions. Cavaliers and Roundheads are the examples which spring most readily to mind, even though the exclusive association of flat crowned broad-brimmed, feather-trimmed hats with Royalist supporters of King Charles I, and plain, untrimmed black conical hats with those of Cromwell and the Parliamentarians owes more to the romantic novelist than it does to the realities, political, social or sartorial of the time.

Below: The crowning of King George V of England of 1911. The Archbishop does not wear his miter.

Above: The crowning of Charles V of France in 1365 as depicted in a late 14th-century manuscript. The bishops wear miters, the king his crown and the nobles in attendance are bare-headed.

By the 18th century, conscious use was being made of the hat as a badge of political identity. During the constitutional struggles in Sweden in 1719–22, the opposing factions were known as Hats and Caps. E. Cobham Brewer in *The Dictionary of Phrase and Fable* (1896), suggests that the explanation lay in the citified Francophile aspirations of the Hat Party and the countrified Russian connections of those who wore the cap. Political associations were also evident in the France of the Revolution. Paris milliners from Rose Bertin downward realized that in such times of heightened political sensitivity, a topical name and a tricoleur rosette would help to sell a hat, but still gave them inimitable 18th-century chic. The Phrygian, the classical Red Cap of Liberty, was the height of fashion for everyone.

The hat retained its political overtones in the 19th century. In Prussia, students, Romantic adherents to what they saw as ancient principles of German liberty, followed the advice of Eric Moritz Arndt in *Ein wort über Sitte, Mode und Kleidertracht* (*A word on Costumes, Fashion and Dress*, 1845); they adopted old German styles, which in their version conveniently and attractively combined floppy frilly shirts and wide-brimmed befeathered hats, in reaction to the severe elegance of their respectable elders, and found themselves the target of Frederick William III and top-hatted authority.

Nevertheless, the wide-brimmed revolutionary hat remained in fashion, its appeal made more popular still by Lajos Kossuth, Hungarian patriot and leader of the movement for independence from Austria, who brought the dashing Kossuth hat to America in his campaigning tour in 1851. Its appeal was reinforced by the successes of Giuseppe Garibaldi in the struggle for Italian independence in 1859, whose irregular forces wore the broad soft hat of the Italian peasant. The top hat, classic men's fashion for all classes for most of the 19th century, had become the "high hat," the hat of authority, with which no aspiring politician would wish to be associated. Bismarck campaigning for the German country vote, wore a wide-brimmed felt, the Demokratenhut. On the other side of the Atlantic, Teddy Roosevelt wore an informal soft hat for his 1912 campaign against President Taft. He was throwing his hat in the ring, so he said, and the hat became his campaign badge.

Beyond the badge of status is the need or desire for a style, and beyond that the creativity of individuals or professional designers and the ingenuity of not one, but several crafts and industries. It is a story which began before written history.

Left: A cap of liberty with a tricoleur cockade. A satirical view of Louis XVI saluting the Revolution in 1792 by P. G. Berthault.

HATS IN THE LANGUAGE

The significance of the hat compared with other articles of clothing is such that it has found its way into many sayings and phrases. Some of these are obsolete, but most have an interesting history behind them, not always easily understood or appreciated today. The list below is not exhaustive but it includes most phrases still in common use, with their meanings, though some still elude complete comprehension:

A bad hat – an objectionable person, a rascal (London Cockney, *c* 1890).

To high–hat – to treat someone superciliously (American); also used in Britain *c* 1930.

Old hat something old, whether it be news or an object (modern use); a whore (18th-century use).

I'll bet a hat – cf. "as by this hat," Shakespeare: to swear by your hat that something is what you say it is.

I'll eat my hat – expression of incredulity, used in early 19th century by Charles Dickens, first in *The Pickwick Papers*.

Brewer in his *Dictionary of Phrase and Fable* (1894) purports to have found a recipe from an 18th-century cookbook: "Hattes are made of eggs, veal, dates, saffron, salt & so forth."

To raise your hat or doff your cap – as a sign of respect men raise their hats one to another and especially to women. Probably a literal survival of the medieval custom of taking off one's helmet or lifting one's visor to recognize and be recognized by one's friends.

To go hat in hand – a servile act, appearing hatless among one's betters, to go to ask or beg for a favor or money.

Hat money – a collection made by passengers in a ship after a good voyage which was then given to the captain. The modern equivalent to a "tip" for the driver or guide at the end of a coach trip.

To pass the hat around – to make a collection; people would drop their money into the hat.

Hat trick – originally to bowl three wickets with three successive balls in a cricket match (1880). It is said that the first time this happened the players were so thrilled they **either** bought the bowler a new hat, **or** passed the hat around and made a collection for him. Today the expression is used for any sporting feat performed three times in succession.

Pulled it out of a hat – to do something suddenly, or unexpectedly, as if by magic; from the act of a conjuror who would make objects appear out of an empty hat.

At the drop of a hat – to do something quickly, even unexpectedly.

To hang up one's hat (in a house) – to make oneself at home. Normally it was polite to hold onto your hat when visiting unless the host asked to take it. Hanging it up yourself was a sign that you "owned the place."

To keep it under your hat – to keep something secret.

To smile under your hat – to be secretly amused.

To talk through one's hat – to talk rubbish.

To be given one's bowler or to be bowler hatted – to be demobilized from the army and exchange a "tin hat" for a civilian one, *c* 1918, mainly in relation to the officer class.

A feather in your cap – a trophy or reward.

Finally, a nearly obsolete but charming old English phrase:

All round my hat! – to be indisposed and based on the old ballad of the man who has lost his sweetheart and so he sings "All round my hat I wear a green willow . . ."

Titfer is a common English slang term for a hat, sometimes spelled titfa or even titva. It derives from the London Cockney rhyming slang in which short phrases are used to describe things; only the first word is usually used, "apples and pears" meaning stairs, but stairs are commonly referred to as apples! "Tit-for-tat" rhymes with hat and is shortened to titfer.

Medieval times

When Charles VII made his triumphal entry into Rouen in 1449, his scarlet hat, with its crimson feather, went down in fashion history, marking the beginning of a new era. After a hundred years of conflict, the French and English were to be at peace although in fashion terms this conflict was to be reenacted many times over the next five centuries. In his speech, Charles is said to have told his followers to exchange their hoods for hats, to abandon faction and conflict for which hoods with badges or distinctive colors were often identification, as well as having utilitarian downmarket and traditional associations. He was encouraging a departure for an age of peace, prosperity, consumerism and fashion.

The felt of which his hat was probably made had a long history. St. Clement, patron saint of felt and hatmakers, is supposed to have invented it on pilgrimage by compressing the wool padding of his sandals. This story is only one of many which attempt to explain a material which is at least as ancient as woven textiles, if not more so, and which worldwide had, and still has, many basic furnishing and clothing uses. As described by J. Tomlinson in the *Encyclopaedia of Useful Arts and Manufacturers* (1854), quoted in M.E. Burkett's valuable *The Art of the Feltmaker* (1979), it is a "non woven material . . . built up of the interlocking of fibres and requires no bonding agent. The fibres become stably intermeshed by a combination of mechanical work, chemical action and heat." It is hard-wearing, weatherproof and its plastic quality makes it very suitable for covering rounded three-dimensional objects, such as heads. Clothing and textiles do not often survive in an archeological context, but the earliest garment so far found in England is a felt hood, perhaps from a hooded cloak of Roman times, the *cucullus*, such as is illustrated by the carved figures from Housesteads on Hadrian's wall.

Hats and headdress as well as felt already had a very long history by the 3rd century A.D. The finds from the Ancient Egyptian tombs illustrate the complexity of techniques, Assyrian bas-reliefs the awe-inspiring height a helmet can give to a warrior, and Greek and Etruscan vase paintings and statuary the variety and charm of the hat in a more peaceful social setting. There is even a painting of a felt workshop at Pompeii. Ancient Greek hats came in several forms: the close-fitting pilos was worn in Greece; the later pileus was the distinguishing mark of a free Roman citizen. The root of the word signifies that they were both made from felt. Basic in style, they may not have been very different from some of the simple felt hats made in the Near East today.

Above: A royal progress as illustrated in the *Grands Chroniques de France* mid-15th century, by Jean Fouquet. Unfortunately, there is no illustration of Charles VIII's entry into Rheims, but here the Constable Robert of Fiennes wears the type of hat worn for traveling, ceremonial as well as useful, with his sash and sword of office, and King Charles his crown.

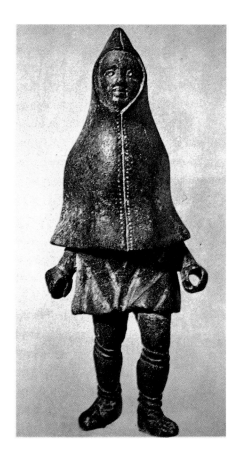

Above: A Roman hooded cloak illustrated by a bronze statuette found in Trier. A possible fragment of a similar garment was found near Hadrian's Wall in Britain.

Above right: A variety of classical Greek headwear as illustrated in Racinet's *Le Costume Historique*.

No actual ancient hats from Europe survive except for those found in Scandinavia. Soil conditions must be suitable for the preservation of archaeological textiles, and finds from the Danish bog burials, as described in E. Munksgaard, *Oldtidsdragter* (1974), show the surprising variety of shapes, and techniques of manufacture of Bronze Age men's caps. From Trindhoff comes a tall cap made from twill woven wool, with the straight brim attached to the crown; and from Muldbjerg, a finely made and sophisticated hemispherical cap, completely covered with a wool pile. The Iron Age man's cap from Tollund is neat and conical with a chin strap, made from eight shaped panels of plain leather, while an example from Celle in north Germany of this period is covered with close-set rows of bronze studs. From Bernuthsfeld in Denmark comes a fur bonnet, close-fitting with chin strap, the panels emphasized with variegated fur. The hairstyles under these caps were also complex and sophisticated, as were those of the women. They wore openwork sprang hair nets and hair arranged over pads. As for the rest of their clothes, the men wore either an enveloping "bean-shaped" cloak or shorter cloak and loincloth, the women a blouse, short strand skirt and possibly a drape worn as a hooded cloak. In the Iron Age there were changes; the men began to wear breeches and shirts and the women a long wider skirt and shawl.

This continuous story of the hat depends on the availability of written and pictorial sources, as well as the occasional artifact, and it is not easy to trace changes in fashion in England and France until the 11th century. Earlier illuminations from manuscripts suggest that comfort and convenience were paramount. With their tunics, hose and cloaks, both men and women wore close caps, usually shown white, and by implication washable. For warmth there were hoods, and for travelling, a hat with a high crown and brim that shaded the eyes; while this was usually worn turned up, it could be turned down to protect the neck. The shape of cap and hood are so dictated by function that there has been,

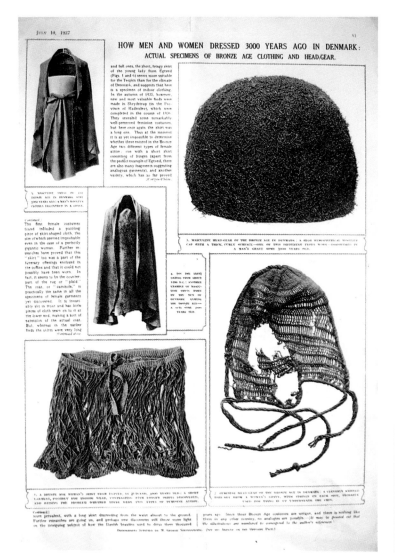

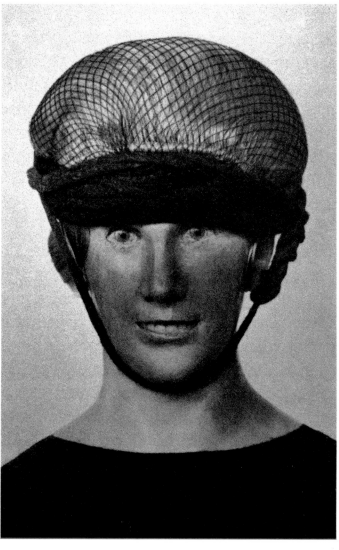

on a basic level, little change in a thousand years. Indeed some shapes are still with us. One feature of the hood that was beginning to alter was the crown; slowly lengthening until it extended into a tail. Many were made with a short cape, the bottom border of which was decoratively treated. Women wore veils loosely over their long braided hair early in the period, though as their coiffure alters and braids begin to be decoratively looped up there are signs of a more contrived arrangement. Possibly the apparent simplicity of what we can see today is a consequence of the technical limitations of the illustrations, for by the 13th century, life was sophisticated and luxurious for the noble and wealthy and the Crusades were bringing luxuries and knowledge from all over the world.

The clothing trades were already specializing; no fewer than nine distinct craftsmen in this area alone are found among the trade and craft associations of the Guilds of Paris, as noted by Etienne Boileau, the Provost of Paris, in his *Livre des Mestiers* (1264). There were the *aumussiers*, who seem to have made hoods involving fur; *chapeliers de cotton* who made cotton hats or caps; the *coiffiers* who made close-fitting caps; *chapeliers de fleurs*, making garlands of real or artificial flowers; the *chapeliers de paon*, making headdresses which featured peacock feathers; *fourreurs de chapeaux*, making fur or fur-trimmed hats; *chapeliers d'orfrois* concerned with jewelled headbands; *chaperonniers* who made hoods, especially the more complicated version then becoming fashionable; and *chapeliers de feûtre* who made felt hats. An exclusively feminine head covering, the veil, was made by the

Above left: Bronze Age outfits from Danish bog burials include (top) a man's cap with needleworked pile finish and (below) a sprang, or single finger-knit hair net.

Above: The hair nets in Bronze Age Denmark were arranged over complex coiffures.

chapeliers de soie, and the *crêpiniers* made the net snoods. Straw hats, like other straw goods, were made by the *nattiers.*

In England, the supply of hats was in the hands of the cappers and hatters who included the hurers, the term coming from the Anglo-Saxon for cap. The London hatters were incorporated by 1348, but it has been suggested that they were concerned mainly with selling hats, many of them imported. They were already complaining about foreign competition as early as 1269.

The hurers made felted shaggy woolen caps with a felted finish. City of London records give some clues about the manufacturing process. Their workshops were probably small and like those of the capmakers in the Middle East today, where the wool is sorted, then beaten, carded and felted through a repeated series of wettings and pressings. The most effective way of arranging the fibers was to use the bow, which was held over the strands of wool and twanged over them until they were all lying in the same orientation, though it is not confirmed that the bow was in use in medieval London. It was known from an early period in the Middle East, but who learned the technique from whom is not known. However it was known in Czechoslovakia by 1418; wall paintings in the Church of St. Egidius at Bedejo Slovakia show it in use.

The tool by which feltmakers and hatters were identified was a stick, about a yard long, and it is with this that they appear in 15th-century Nuremberg guild portraits and in Jost Ammans' 16th-century illustrations of the crafts. This tool was used both for beating the wool to soften it, and for getting rid of loose hairs on the finished hats.

The work of compressing the fibers was tedious and hard, though it is on this crucial process that the waterproof finish and the quality of the cap depend. In the Middle East there were two methods, using the hands or the feet, or both, but the English hurers were insistent that caps ". . . cannot and ought not to be fulled under the feet or in any other way than by the hands of men." The bad

Below: A hood and tunic of the later 13th century, from an illuminated manuscript.

Left: A courtly riding party from the *Très Riches Heures du Duc de Berry,* illuminated by the Limburg brothers in the early 15th century. The man wears a chaperon-draped hood, the women wide padded bourrelets, or veils supported with wires.

workmanship of one John Godwyne, is commemorated in Riley's *Memorials of Old London.* As a pinner, or interloper, he was in any case suspect, but he was also incompetent. His caps, it seems, were inadequately fulled, "falsely and deceitfully made," and were also "oiled with grease that was rank and putrid, by reason whereof they stank." But a new technology was tempting. Water-powered fulling mills had been introduced in the 12th century, though for woolen cloth in the piece, but some bright hurer must have realized their potential, because in 1376 there are complaints that caps fulled in the mills were tearing the lengths of cloth and spoiling its smooth finish. Undaunted, the hurers set up their own mills; this time their brethren in the trade complained of overcharging and poor quality control and supervision!

Almost as a last resort it would seem, some took themselves off to the banks of the Thames to ply their craft, but this time they scandalized their city neighbors. A complaint in autumn 1398 notes that "to the great scandal . . . of the good folks of the said trade of the City," they had sent children to do the work "amid horrible tempests, frosts and snows," though they were not too weak to make trouble with the servants of the nobility using Thames bank to water the horses. In a conflict between hats and horses, the journeymen and apprentices of the hurers were "wrangling . . . and on the point of killing one another."

It is a pity one has no idea of the quality end of the trade, other than through the Masterpiece regulations of the Paris *bonnetiers* as late as 1609, although by that time they were obviously outdated. They brought their own wool with them, and the quality was important because if it was too coarse, or from sheep sheared at the wrong season, or from dead or diseased sheep, it would not take colors

Above: Many types of headdress can be seen in the varied scenes that make up this 15th-century altarpiece, *The Martyrdom of St. Barbara.* The men's hats, especially those with high crowns, may be of felt, but others with turned-up brims may have been of fur.

Above: A felt hat-making workshop in Shiraz, Iran, in the late 1960s suggests the scale and methods probably used in medieval times. The man and boy are felting the hoods by damping and rolling them. The finished hats are visible in the background.

well. Using two pounds of wool, and working before their guild brethren, the would-be hatters fulled and shaped a cap, formerly called an almuce, and two cremiolles, said to be round with a turned-up brim. Slightly more up-to-date and upmarket was the square cap which they had to make and block, as well as one of pleated velvet.

Nevertheless, even in the 14th century, the goods were many and varied. Riley's *Memorials* tell us that in 1311 a hatter had 40 gray and white hats in stock, and 15 black hats, and in 1418, a hurer was working on 6 double round hats, 18 long caps, 6 children's long caps and 24 single or striped round caps.

The illustrations depict the great and the good almost exclusively and rarely show the people who wore obviously basic, everyday caps. Moreover the scale is too small to distinguish woven from felted or knitted caps. It has been suggested by Alfred Franklin in *La vie Privée d'autrefois: Les Magasins de Nouveauté,* (1905) that the *bonnetiers*, who made the white head-hugging caps were, by the 14th century, having them knitted. The earliest English reference to knitted caps comes from Coventry guild records, a century later.

Far more stylish and expensive were the hats. Native English hats were made of wool felt and though this was often dyed, white, gray and black were the usual colors. However, by 1323, quality was much improved when the Paris *chaperonniers*, until then confined to using only lamb's wool, were specifically allowed to use beaver. This made a lustrous, malleable and waterproof felt and above all a light one, because wool felt hats were probably quite heavy to wear. The beaver frontier of North America was still far beyond the flat medieval horizon, but there was a plentiful local supply of the animals, from which it is said, a river near

Paris, the Bièvre, took its name. Pelts were also imported from Russia and northern Europe. The Low Countries were the hub of manufacture and it is a beaver hat from Flanders that Geoffrey Chaucer's rich merchant wears for his Canterbury pilgrimage in 1386.

Beaver hats were worn by women as well as men and were the height of fashion at the French court. In the trousseau of Blanche de Bourbon, who married Pedro of Castille in 1352, there was a hat of scarlet velvet and beaver embroidered with gold, pearls and precious stones, with a lively design of children gathering chestnuts in a flower-filled garden. Overhead fly birds, and at their feet deer and pigs nibble the fallen nuts. Undoubtedly expensive, the hat appears in an inventory of jewelry. Edward III is described by Froissart as having hats of beaver and "oestryddes feathers" and in the inventory of Sir John Fastolf, a tough elderly soldier-administrator who died in 1459 and who is said to have been the inspiration for Shakespeare's Falstaff, there is a single beaver hat, lined with damask and with a gilt girdle, the hatband.

Hats of more basic quality were worn by ordinary people, and from illuminated manuscripts appear to be similar in shape to the petasos worn for traveling in Ancient Greece. Broad-brimmed with a low crown, sometimes with a knob on the top perhaps a relic of the making process and with tying strings, they survive as the cardinal's hat. The ordinary traveling hat resembles in style the type we associate with popular representations of Robin Hood. It had a brim to shade the eyes or turned up at the back. Souvenir pilgrim badges such as cockleshells were popular decorations. Throughout the period, a hat is used consistently in illustrations to identify the Jew. Usually yellow, it has a concave curve and is surmounted by a sort of pinnacle, but the dress regulations relating to their status as aliens and unbelievers do not specify the material of which they were made.

In the early 14th century, as the fashion line elongated, so the crown of the hat began to rise, a feature which could be emphasized by the arrangement of the jewel, badge or feather which often trimmed the front. Some were tall and stiff enough to resemble the top hats of Victorian days. By the early 15th century, there were signs that breadth was to be an important feature of fashion. Sleeves bulked larger and the waistband began to fall to a natural level. Balancing this new line, hats became lower with crowns wide rather than deep, and with heavy turned-up brims. It is much easier to appreciate the quality of the materials in the larger-scale panel paintings which now become increasingly useful as a source of information. Thus in Jan van Eyck's *The Arnolfini Marriage* (1434) we can appreciate the texture of Nicolas Arnolfini's splendidly massive hat.

The most basic headcovering was the hood, also known in England as the amess and in France as the amuce, which has, as the amice, continued in ecclesiastical usage. In England and France it was also known as the chaperon. It could be made in any material and in single or mixed colors. The color of the hood could be important because it often signified an allegiance. The followers of Charles VII of France wore a white cross on their hoods, those of rebellious merchant Etienne Marcel red and blue. The colors of a woman's hood could also be significant, and in an early English sumptuary ordinance of 1342, prostitutes were supposed to identify themselves by wearing red and white striped hoods.

Danish bogs reveal a little as to how hoods might have been made. In the late 14th century, a man traveling through Bochsten in south Sweden was murdered, probably garotted, a stake thrust through his heart, and his corpse tossed into a ditch. With his fitted woolen tunic and hose he wore a hood with a cape. It has a deep cowl with turned-back front opening, a shaped headpiece hood from the back of which dangled a tippet or liripipe, a seamed tapering tail of material long enough to reach to the small of the back. There is a contrasting border at the front

**Right: Jews can usually be
identified in Western European
medieval illustrations by their
distinctive hats, prescribed by
13th-century German
ordinances. In this group from
the Leipzig Machsor of the late
13th century, the priest is
enveloped in a prayer shawl;
the others wear the "Jewish
hat."**

**Above: The portrait of
Nicolas Arnolfini and his wife
by Jan van Eyck, 1434, shows
them in formal high bourgeois
fashion. Despite the precision
of the detail, it is not possible
to be certain of the materials
from which Nicolas
Arnolfini's hat is made, but
research on the veil worn by
his wife, folded diagonally,
suggests that the crimped edges
were woven with fluted effect.
She wears it over hair arranged
and netted into peaks at the
temples.**

opening of the shoulder-length cape. The pattern, published in M. Nockert's
Bochstensmannen Och Hans Drakt (1985), shows it to have been cut across the
width of the fabric, and stitched only down the back. It was a warm well-fitted
garment. But the hood had its inconveniences; a comfort in cold weather, it
would have been a nuisance in the heat. Etiquette also demanded that it be doffed
in the presence of social superiors, instantly ruining a neat and fashionable
hairstyle. The long tippet might have been used as a pocket, but it is a feature of
doubtful utility and was probably inconvenient. As collars rose higher in the
mid-13th century, the cape below the hood became superfluous.

By the mid-14th century, the cape-hood was restyled to suit the more fitted
and structured line of the clothing, and the doublet with the high band collar
which by then had become fashionable. Instead of being drawn over the head, it
is perched on it with the face-opening, or gule, used as a headband and eventually
stiffened and padded, while cape and liripipe are twisted into an approximation of
a turban form. Originally spontaneous variations, they soon began to be stitched
into a number of ingenious shapes. Some of them have the decoratively cut-out
edge of the cape forming almost a coxcomb effect. The wardrobe of Sir John
Fastolf gives some idea of their relative popularity in the wardrobe. He had the
beaver hat already mentioned, two straw hats, a knit cap and 28 hoods, the most
splendid a "Hood of scarlet with a roll of purple velvet bordered with the same; a
hood of russet velvet the tippet lined with russet silk; a hood of russet damask
with the tippet fastened with a lace of silk." Colorful as they were, they pale
before that of King John of France, described by Etienne de La Fontaine as being
made from two shades of scarlet cloth embroidered in gold and pearls with wild
men and animals.

Women also wore *chaperons*. Jeanne de Bourbon, wife of the French King
Charles VII had at least 11 richly decorated examples in her wardrobe. The Duke
of Burgundy's New Year gift to the Duchess in 1371 was embroidered with 600
large pearls and 50 ounces of seed pearls. The *chaperons* of ordinary ladies were

obviously not of this standard; indeed ostentation outside the nobility was never approved and in the early 16th century, French bourgeoises were restricted by sumptuary law to wearing black and scarlet cloth only.

It is with her headdress that the medieval lady makes her most unforgettable even assertive fashion statement. Ecclesiastical criticism mounted in proportion to the size of headdress, its venom explicable in the context of a male-dominated society in which women were supposed to be meek and subordinate, their role conforming to Judeo-Christian ideology; long hair, an essential attribute of the conventional woman, had to be concealed, modestly draped, and as far as possible invisible. Michael Harrison in *The History of the Hat* (1967), suggests that the root of the word "wife" is "veiled", though this is not confirmed in the current *Oxford English Dictionary*; however, Chaucer's Wife of Bath (1386), dominant and extrovert, traveling "with her hat as broode as is a bokeler or a targe," was probably ruefully recognized as typical rather than exceptional.

The mid-15th-century lady, head held high, a towering figure crowned with gleaming sweeping horns, her face framed rather than concealed by a diaphanous veil was an ostentatious and aggressive figure. Dom Lydgate no doubt spoke for many when he wrote "Beauty wol showe, thogh hornes wer away" and that "Hornes were given to beastys ffor defence . . . to be made sturdy of resystance; while for women such was a thing contrarie."

The social dimension of fashion is brought out in the sumptuary legislation. One of its aims was to restrict people to clothes proper to their class. In the English Statute of Apparel (1360), for instance, wives of yeomen were restricted

Above: Peat bog preserved the woolen clothing of a man murdered in the late 13th-century in Bochsten, Sweden. The hood, almost perfectly preserved, has liripipe and a short shoulder cape with contrasting yellow front decoration.

Left: Louis of Anjou wears his hood twisted into a turban shape. The cape, with a decorative cut edge, can be seen dangling over the forehead; the painting is from the mid-15th century.

to yarn of English manufacture and the servant class to an expenditure of 12 pence for their veils. But in general the upper classes, the nobility, had the right to, as well as the means for, ostentation, though the constant reenactments show how often these regulations were breached by the merely wealthy and ambitious. The regulation of something as amorphous as a hairstyle was impossible and the hellfire sermons of Friar Richard and Thomas Connecte were directed as much at the uppity bourgeoisie as at the immodest nobility.

The basic headdress of the mature and married woman until the 12th century was a veil covering hair arranged in pendant braids. Sometimes referred to as a headrail, it seems to have been rectangular, kept in place with a fillet and worn with the straight narrow border drooped down over the forehead. It could be colored as well as white. There is little change until the end of the 12th century when the veil was draped or held back with a band to show more of the face and the long plaited locks. As an alternative to the fillet, a barbette might be worn which covered the sides of the head, cheeks and ears. Even more enveloping was the wimple, a light covering for the neck and chest, drawn up at the side of the face to the temples. Always a fashion for the mature, long after it had ceased to be in general use, it continued to be worn by widows in mourning dress.

By the 13th century, the style of hairdressing had changed. Instead of letting the braids hang loose, the ladies knotted them above the ears, covering the hair at the temples with a caul. A short veil at the back of the head was more decorative than modest. By the end of the 14th century, the coiled plaits at the side stood proud of the head. They were sometimes not entirely of their owner's own growing, and, according to Juvenal des Ursins, might include the hair of the dead

Right: Women's headdress in the 11th century seems to have consisted of a simple veil. An illustration from the book of Isaiah from the Lambeth Bible.

and the damned. The Knight of de la Tour Landry who wrote his elegant moral tale in 1374, subsequently translated into English by William Caxton, noted with disapproval that women were so avid of novelty that with their headdresses they looked like "snaile deer or unicors," while they were "attyred with high long pynnes lyke a gebet [gibbet] bore a galous [gallows] on her head." The structures grew larger and more fantastic and began to spread horizontally rather than vertically. It was a period of wealth and ostentation in England and Burgundy, though less so in France proper, which had been hugely impoverished in the Hundred Years' War. Fashion was sensitive to influences from abroad and turban shapes reflected the contacts with the Near East. The high headdresses are said to have been introduced by Anne of Bohemia, Richard II's Queen in the late 14th century.

There was a sustained reaction to fashionable ostentation at the beginning of the 15th century led by traveling preachers. In 1429, according to the "Bourgeois de Paris," a sermon by Friar Richard persuaded the ladies to burn their vanities, their veiled headdresses, the leather and the whalebone with which they stiffened and shaped their *chaperons*. In 1432, the campaign was continued by the Breton Friar Connecte. He employed ridicule, inciting boys to pursue the ladies, pull down their headdresses, calling *"heurte Bellin"* ("beware of the ram") or *"Au hennin,"* probably translatable as "Donkey" and a reference to the resemblance to asses' ears. It worked, according to Monstrelet; the ladies adopted caps like the peasants or nuns, but only briefly, for "this reform lasted not long, for like as snails when any one passes by them draw in his horns and when all danger seems over put them in again . . . so these ladies began to resume their former colossal

Below: Christine de Pisan in the 1430s presents her manuscript to the Duchess who, like her ladies, wears a wide padded bourrelet headdress, under which can be seen the cap on which it is mounted and decorative knots of hair at the temples. A loop on the forehead provides additional support, and there is a short veil at the back. The tall white headdress such as Christine de Pisan wears appears to have been a veil folded into a triangle, with the diagonal draped around the hair at the back and the spare material supported on tall wires at the temple and then folded back. It should be compared with the arrangement of the veil in the Arnolfini portrait.

Right: The headdress at its highest is to be seen in this illustration by Loyset Liedet and Guillaume Vrelant for *L'Hystoire de Helayne,* 1443–48. The queen wears a crown over her pointed blue hat and her mother-in-law a veil supported on long angled wires which can be seen at the apex. The other ladies wear the steeple headdress. The fold marks of the veil are a feature. The men's hats are tall and pointed and the Duke of Gloucester's is surmounted by a beret-like tuft. The older men in the background wear chaperons and long robes.

headdresses and wore them even higher than before."

The headdress had risen to extraordinary heights by the third quarter of the 15th century. The ladies wore towering conical caps with loops at the forehead for support, and twin peaks with wires supporting veils like butterfly wings. Hennin and gibet seem to be used descriptively as terms for the high headdresses; sophisticated, snide comment at the ecclesiastical disapproval. By the end of the 15th century, the fashion line changed decisively. The waist was lowered and to compensate, the headdress shrank. The former towering cap became a mere support for a turned-back veil, almost as enveloping and more rigid than it had been 300 years before, beginning a course of development it was to follow during the 16th century as a hood. It is possibly significant that in a century that would include the age of Elizabeth, the headdress was to emphasize a woman's face and not distract from it. The sympathetic skill of the great portraitists of the time, Dürer, Holbein, and the Van Eycks was to record a speaking, thinking likeness as well as realistic details of the headdress which framed and enhanced it.

Left: The tall steeple headdress of the third quarter of the 15th century is worn by the ladies in the presentation before the tournament in the Book of Hours of King René. The tall caps with pendant veils and dark hoods are also worn.

Above: By the end of the 15th century, headdresses were low and many women wore simple black hoods and the men small caps, as seen in this round dance from *Le Roman de la Rose.*

The sixteenth century

It is conventional to schedule modern times as beginning in the 16th century; the hat, like so much else, would never be the same again. The beaver frontier of the New World had been breached; the hat of the Renaissance plutocrat, the beaver, or the castor, would soon be within reach of the ordinary man. The concept of the hat as a consumer durable began to alter, and the competition for raw material, furs for felt, was to have a dramatic effect on international relations and ultimately to shape the history of America and its frontiers.

The fur trade, which supplied the Netherlands with the raw material from which the much prized beaver felts were processed, was described by Adriaan van der Donck, an experienced fur trader. The methods he wrote about in the mid-17th century, were probably equally true of the trade's beginnings in the 16th century:

> From the fur of the beaver the best hats are made . . . they are called beavers or castoreums from the material . . . and are known all over Europe. The outer coat is of a chestnut brown color, the browner the color the better is the fur . . . When the hats are made . . . the rough hairs are pulled out for they are useless. The skins are usually first sent to Russia where they are greatly valued for their outside shining hair . . . The skins are used for mantle linings . . . Therefore we call the same Peltries . . . after the hairs have fallen out, or are worn, and . . . become old and dirty and apparently useless, we get the article back, and convert the fur into hats, before which it cannot be well used for this purpose, for unless the beaver has been worn, and is greasy and dirty, it will not felt properly, hence these old peltries are the most valuable. The coats which the Indians make of beaver skins and which they have worn for a long time about their bodies until the skins have become fould with perspiration and grease are afterwards used by hatters and make the best hats.

In each beaver skin, therefore, there was a double profit, and it is a sad tribute to the ability of the beaver to survive that it was not until the 1920s that it was classed as an endangered animal. Fortunately, the hunting methods of the Native Americans the main hunters of the skins, were traditionally conceived to perpetuate the survival of the species.

The hub of the fur trade in France was at La Rochelle in the Vendée, south of Britanny, the coast from which the first French explorers had set out for the New

Above right: The beaver and a microscopic view of one of its hairs showing the notched construction which made it so well adapted to felting; from a mid-19th-century engraving.

Below: A Russian nobleman of the 17th century in the fur-trimmed robes which when worn out were the raw material for the early fur felt hat industry.

World. The fishing boats went to the Grand Banks off Newfoundland regularly and what had been Codfish Land became the beaver frontier, as they enhanced their profits by trading with the Indians for pelts, and returned loaded with fish and increasingly with "diverse sortes of fine furs." Hakluyt (1598), the English geographer, noted in one man's house "Canadian otter and beaver to the value of 5000 crowns."

In England, the beaver skins from the New World were traded in the profitable fur markets in the City of London. There felt-makers were poised to take advantage of this raw material, having learned new methods from immigrant felt-makers from Rheims. These religious refugees had left France at the beginning of the 16th century and settled in Southwark by 1517. The felt-makers sought separation from the Haberdashers' Company with whom they had become associated, but did not achieve their independence until 1604. The trade had obvious potential which was to be more fully exploited in the 17th century, as styles changed and felt replaced fabric hats.

The fashions of the first half of the 16th century emphasized the breadth of the figure, square and substantial with sleeves broad at shoulder and upper arm, and with the waist at low natural level. A loose gown was often worn. The massive grandeur of the really fashionable is best seen in the paintings of Holbein. Hats were small, confirming rather than attempting to counterbalance the line. Dress across Europe was diverse, with many national variants even at fashionable level. A popular form of hat of the early 16th century was flat and worn level and high on the head, with a deep soft crown almost covering the brim, which was generally worn turned up. The caps of the Yeomen of the Guard, the Beefeaters of the Tower of London, are based on styles of the reign of Henry VIII. The brim was sometimes split into sections and it was possible to vary the arrangement to shield eyes, ears or nape. A popular version, the Milan bonnet, is said to have had a notably deep, upturned brim. When this was much deeper than the crown was high, it gave a halo effect if turned up. Badges or jewels were popular trimmings, as were feathers. Part decorative and part functional were the laces or aiglets, which could be used to tie up flaps. They were found particularly on German examples, and were used to trim the hats with great profusion. By the 1530s, the

Above: A cap-maker's workshop from Jost Amman's *Book of Trades,* 1569. On the right, the caps are being felted and shaped over a barrel of heated water. In the middle, the other worker beats them to soften them and to detach the loose hairs, and another shears them. Those completed are ranged on the shelves at the back and appear to have a textured surface.

Above: Henry VIII by Hans Holbein, 1536. The king wears the flat beret-like, jewel-studded and feather-trimmed cap which complements the fashionable breadth of his outfit.

Right: Beefeaters today at the Tower of London still wear the flat wide-brimmed hats with hat-bands that they wore in the days of Henry VIII.

Above: Three young German women of *c*1528–30, painted by Lucas Cranach the Elder, wearing magnificent feather-trimmed caps with upturned brims over decorative hair nets. The hairstyle which they covered can be seen on the left.

hat was worn more frequently at an acute angle. As in previous centuries, it was often worn over a cap and also a decorative net or caul, anticipating the dolly hats of the 1930s and 1940s. They were worn by women as well as men. Again, the German examples were particularly elaborate and can be clearly seen in paintings by Lucas Cranach.

By the second half of the 16th century, the crown had become more important than the brim. Fashion had begun to stress height rather than breadth. Some hats were made from felt, others were possibly faced or trimmed with silk, as John Shelton wrote in *The Way of the World* (1540): "Nowadays so many painted caps, Lased with double flaps, And so gay felted caps saw I never." The disapproving eye is always the most observant and the best account of contemporary fashion comes from Philip Stubbes, Puritan divine and censor of morals in his *Anatomie of Abuses* (1586, and reprinted several times). In the dress of Aelgna (thinly disguised England), after having recorded his disapproval of those who dressed above their station, and the padded attenuated lines of the fashion of the period, he noted:

Hatts of Sundrie Fations . . . Sometimes they use them sharp on the Crowne, pearking up like a Sphere, or Shafte of a Steeple, standing a quarter of a yarde above the Crowne of their heades . . . Othersome be flat and broad on the Crowne like the battlements of a house. An other sort have rounde Crownes, sometimes with one kinde of Bande, sometimes with another . . . never content with one colour or fashion two dayes to an ende . . . the thinges whereof their hattes be made diverse also; for some are Silke, some of Velvet, some of Taffatie, some of Sarenet, some of Wooll, . . . a Velvet or a Taffatie hatte . . . must be Pincked and Cunnyngly Carved. And good profitable

hattes be these, for the longer you weare them the fewer holes they have . . . and another sorte are content with no kinde of hat without a great Bunche of Feathers . . . peakyng on toppe of their heades, not unlyke I dare not saie Cockescombes, but as sternes of pride and ensignes of vanitie. . . . many get good liuving by dying and selling of them and not a few prouve themselves more than Fooles in wearyng of them.

Beaver is also mentioned as "more curious, some of a certaine kinde of fine Hair; these they call Bever hattes, . . . fetched from beyonde the seas . . . " Obviously it was considered a popular, if expensive, import. Included among his tall hats may have been the copontain, which in Junius Nomenclator 1585 is described as "a heade with a sharpe crowne . . . like a sugar loaf." Many happily shocked at his satirical exposé of modern styles were relatively uninvolved. The usual wear of tradesmen and artisans was the flat cap, and Flatcap was a common name for an apprentice. The shape was not much changed from what it had been at the beginning of the century, though just a little broader in the crown.

The cap had advantages, still apparent when Decker set them out in *The Honest Whore* (1634): "light in summer and in cold it sits close to the skull . . . It shows the whole face boldly. . . . Flat caps as proper are to city gowns as to armour helmets, or to kings their crowns." They were often colored: red, green, blue and black are all mentioned. Some were made of felt, but many were knitted and then felted. Thomas Fuller calls them "the most warme and profitable coverings of men's heads in the Island" and writes that they afforded occupations to 15 different trades. Cap-making was regarded as an important national craft. The basic yarn had to be carded and spun; then there were the knitters, and for fulling

Above: A cross-section of English society is enjoying itself at the Horsleydown marriage feast painted by Joris Hofnaegel in the 1560s. City and townsfolk, men and women, wear similar hats all with high crowns. The coifs worn by many of the women under their hats, and seen uncovered in the middle group, might be compared with those worn by the Dutch women a century later in the painting by Jan Steen. The flat cap is worn by the older men. Wide-brimmed traveling hats are also visible on heads and suspended over shoulders.

Above: The tall hat, almost like a top hat in shape, complements the comparatively plain outfit worn by the melancholy young man painted by Isaac Oliver at the end of the 16th century.

Above right: The elegantly attenuated fashionable line of the late 16th century, as worn by Sir Jeremy Bowes, is enhanced and elongated with the tilted cap, trimmed with jeweled buttons and feathers.

the wool, partiers of wool, forcers, thicksters, dressers, walkers and dyers; for blocking and finishing, batelliers, shearers; and for the finishing, pressers, edgers and liners, and for trimming, the band-makers.

The knitting method has been analyzed by Richard Rutt, Bishop of Coventry, in his *History of Knitting* (1988). The tension varied from 15 to 24 or 28 stitches to 4 inches. The caps seem to have been knitted either from the top, in the case of a close-fitting skull cap, or from the underside of the brim, for a flat cap. There is little technical difference between those from the *Mary Rose*, sunk in 1547, and others dated later; after all, they were professionally made. For example, the Coventry cappers, who had existed as a separate trade from the mid-13th century and were incorporated in 1424, included knitters by 1465. Another center for cap-making was Monmouth on the Welsh borders, where Monmouth caps, known colloquially as "Welsh Wigs," were being made from the 1520s. Close-fitting, warm, waterproof and thick, they were popular with sailors and soldiers and are still made as a folk craft today. They were, however, quite expensive and in the 1629 list of supplies recommended for colonists by the Governor and Company of Massachusetts are "5 knit caps milled about 5d [pence] per piece" (these were probably quite simple and plain) "and two Monmouth caps costing two shillings each."

Despite their advantages it seems that by the last quarter of the century, there were fears that all was not well with the trade, though whether the threat came from fashion, over-flashy socially indistinguishable artisans, or from cheap imported caps or wool is not clear. Perhaps all of these were contributory factors. In 1571, in the Statute of Apparel, the last in the series of sumptuary laws, parliament decreed that all above the age of 6 except the nobility or "other persons of degree had on Sabbath and Holydays to wear caps of wool manufactured in England." One of those fined under this law was Shakespeare's uncle; the law was rescinded in 1597.

Fortunately, a reasonable number of caps survive in museums, for many have been found in Tudor rubbish pits and the wool resists the acid London soil very well. There is also the large collection from the *Mary Rose*, Henry VIII's unfortunate warship, and these have the advantage of being precisely datable.

Caps of a very different kind, embroidered nightcaps worn indoors and

Above: An English late 16th-century cap, knitted and fulled. Known as the flat cap, it was government-regulation wear for middle-ranking men. This example was found in the City of London.

Left: An interesting flat felt cap worn by the Count of Lowenstein, in a portrait by H. Baldung (Grien), 1513. The utilitarian earflaps have become merely decorative; the jewel is emblematic and the chin strap is an unusual feature.

Above: Many embroidered caps similar to that worn by Phineas Pett, master shipbuilder, in this anonymous portrait of 1612, survive. Upmarket informal wear in the late 16th and early 17th centuries, they are made from linen and are often richly embroidered and seem to have become family heirlooms.

Right: The family of Sir Thomas More, a miniature copied from the subsequently amended painting of 1526 by Hans Holbein. The women wear English hoods, some with the side drapes pinned up, and French hoods. Sir Thomas wears a biretta, or flat cap, and his father an unusually tall hat.

fashionable through the early 1600s, are also frequently found in museums. From the number surviving, they must have been prestige gifts. Made of linen, though occasionally of satin, they are based on a series of panels that curve in toward the top of the crown and have a deep, closely furled brim. The embroidery is usually fine and many have designs based on the simple scrolls and flowers, birds and insects that also appear in the many popular printed pattern books of the time.

At the beginning of the 16th century, women were wearing clothes which to our eyes are much more restrained than the fashions of the greater part of the 15th century. The extreme vertical emphasis of the 1480s was replaced by a lower waisted line which, as in the case of the men, is confirmed by a low headdress. For very formal occasions, a transparent veil was draped over a truncated cone, standing slightly above the crown of the head. All the hair was scraped back to be concealed under the austere line of the headdress. The variety we know best from portraits and effigies had a shoulder-length hood with the front either rounded or supported into a peak in the middle of the forehead, a line familiar from the queens depicted on conventional playing cards. The hood was supported on what looks like a truncated cone and its cape is slit at the side, making it easier to wear. At the front of the hood and at the temple was a decorative lining. Velvet was popular and often black.

The headdress seems rigid and formalized, and has been immortalized by a painter of genius, Hans Holbein. The drawings and paintings from his years at the court of Henry VIII illustrate it in all its varieties, formal and informal. There are hoods with the cape now split into lappets and little more than rectangular pendants turned up on one or both sides, draping over the top of the gable. The front hair has disappeared entirely, wrapped in contrast fabric and placed across the forehead. The back of the undercap has been squared off and it is now little more than a pillbox sometimes held on with a ribbon under the chin.

More youthful-looking was the alternative, the French hood. This was rounded, with a decorative, often jeweled, border, the *billement* around the edge. At the back, the hood had become little more than a narrow curtain. A particular

variant with a straight border at the brow was associated with Queen Mary I. Informally, a plain white cap was sometimes worn, perhaps little more than a kerchief folded into a triangle and placed over a stiff inner support or undercap to which it was pinned. The fur lettice cap (from lettues or lettwis, a grey squirrel) of similar gabled shape must have been snug in cold weather, and in the sun, there was the bongrace, a rectangular panel pinned to the undercap, stiffened and projecting forward to shade the eyes.

Early in the 15th century, the Countess of Richmond, the mother of Henry VII, had set down the regulations for court mourning modified according to rank. Common to the dress prescribed for ladies was an enveloping headdress which involved a black hood, white inner cap and barbe, a form of wimple. This dress was simplified in the 16th century, but a pointed projection, the beck, recalls the veil of the previous era. Mary Queen of Scots, widowed for the first time in 1560 and again in 1567, wore a wired mourning veil, a shadow and a close-fitting cap with a point on the forehead. The fashion was French, and the widow's peak as worn by her remained a feature of the ritual mourning costume for a widow until the 20th century.

In the second half of the century, the change is less in the lines and types of head-coverings than in the ways of wearing them. The hair began to be built up on the forehead and became a feature, and the hood worn further back was sometimes wired to follow the curve. The lines of an undercap or caps can sometimes be seen, neatly pinned in place. Some informal caps were embroi-

Above left: An English gentlewoman of the late 1520s by Hans Holbein, a brush drawing in ink tinted with wash, shows her wearing an English hood, of which there are two views. It consists of a decorative cover for the hair at the forehead, an undercap probably wired to curve away from the cheeks, and a decorative overcap with flaps turned up and pinned at the sides, to which is attached a square pillbox with rectangular "curtains."

Above: Lady Jane Grey, in a 1546 painting by Master John, wears a French hood, bejeweled and stiffened to frame the face and with a black curtain-like veil at the back.

Right: The lady called the
Countess of Somerset, in this
early 17th-century miniature
by Isaac Oliver, wears an
embroidered cap or forehead
cloth below her wired gauze
veil, or "shadow."

Right: An English coif or cap
and forehead cloth of the late
16th century or early 17th
century. It is made of linen
embroidered with silks,
spangles and metal thread. The
cap would fit neatly with slight
gathering at the crown to
accommodate the hair, which
was arranged in a bun. The
triangular forehead cloth may
have been an optional addition
or alternative.

dered, the delicacy of the design enhanced rather than masked by a gauzy cover. A large number of such caps survive, with patterns similar to those on the men's nightcaps. The shape is simple, a rectangle stitched down the back and with gathered fulness at the crown to accommodate the knot of hair. At the nape is a draw tape or cord to adjust the fulness, as they do not seem to have been tied under the chin. The fronts are sometimes curved forward at the cheeks so that they could be flared out over the side puffs of hair. The purpose of the triangular forehead cloths is less clear since no portraits show their precise arrangement. The only clue comes from 18th-century baby layettes where in unaltered doll arrangements, probably reproducing earlier fashions, a similar triangle can be seen between inner and outer cap with its point backward tied with tapes under the back of the head.

The customs of married and unmarried women differed according to Herman von Meteren, a German traveler in 1575: " . . . married women only wear a hat both in the street and without; those unmarried go without a hat . . . " For those who did wear hats, Stubbes had noticed on:

> their goodly heads . . . their other capitall ornaments, as French hood, hat, cap, kercher, and suche like, where of some be of velvet, some of taffatie, some (but few) of woll, some of this fashion, some of that, and some of this colour, some of that, according to the variable fantasies of their serpentine minds. And to such excesse is it growen as every artificers wyfe (almost) will not stick to goe in her hat of velvet every day, every marchants wyfe and meane gentlewoman in her French hood, and everye poore, cottagers daughter in her taffatie hat, or els of woll at least, well lined with silk, velvet or taffatie.

In contrast to this, some women, especially the young and unmarried girls, "Golden heads fraught with leaden wit," wore no covering for their head, except:

> cawles, made netwyse, to th'ende, as I thinke, that the cloth of gold, clothe of silver or else tinsell (for that is the worst) wherewith the heads are covered and attyred with all underneath then cawles may appeare . . . so that a man that seethe them (there heads glisten and shine in suche sorte) wold thinke them to

have golden heads.

A class-conscious 16th-century Puritan, concerned for the consumption of England's staple woolen cloth, Stubbes finally thunders to a conclusion:

> But how they come by this (so they have it) they care not, who payeth for it they regard not . . . Thus lavishe they foorth the goods of the Lorde . . . upon pride and nautinesse, delighting (as it seemeth) in nothing so much as in the stincking puddle of vanitie and slime, which will be their own decay at last.

Above: A lady painted in 1569 wears a neat beret-like cap, studded with gold buttons and trimmed with a curling ostrich feather.

Above right: Lady Kitson by George Gower, 1573. She wears a high crowned unisex hat, probably made from fabric over a felt foundation, trimmed with a jeweled hatband and a curled feather.

Right: Mrs. John Croker, by George Gower, *c*1580, wears a rich hat, probably made of velvet, bejeweled and trimmed with feathers, and wired up to follow the line of her hair. It should be compared with those worn in the De Bruyn plate.

QUEEN ELIZABETH'S WARDROBE

Queen Elizabeth's wardrobe was to provide the definitive fashion survey of the later 16th century; this has been listed and annotated by J. Arnold in *Queen Elizabeth's Wardrobe Unlocked* (1988). It gives a unique opportunity to personalize fashion, a dimension too often missing from historical sources. The storehouse warrants and bills and the inventory detail clothes worn by a Queen who could be judged media conscious and dressed the part as monarch of a thrusting, nouveau riche smallish state very conscious of a growing role in world politics. At the same time it is the collection of a single lady aware of her charm, thrifty, generous to her friends and expecting more than reciprocal recognition in kind. There are clothes for all occasions, private, public, indoor, outdoor, for duty, leisure and pleasure. A couture milliner having appreciated the worldly position of a client would at the same time be assessing her appearance. Judging from portraits and those observant letter writers, the Venetian ambassadors, Queen Elizabeth knew how to dress and made the best of her looks. She was above average height, slim when young, heavier in middle years, graceful and with good posture. She had clear pale skin, hazel eyes and hair in youth, red gold hair, replaced with red wigs as it thinned.

Many of the hats ordered are black, as are the hoods. The glory was in the hatbands, which were often jeweled, the linings pinked for contrast of texture, the feathers ostrich or egret, sometimes in combination and trimmed with sequins. They took about one and a half yards of 20-inch material to make up, satin or velvet mounted over felt. The hoods required a similar amount. However only one hat from among many survived to be included in the inventories made after her death. Its trimming was so precious that it was classified as jewelry; "one Cappe of black vellat with a bande haveinge ten buttons of gold whereof fyve are set with Cinques of sparkes of diamondes and fower small pearles in a peece, the other fyve with fower sarkes of rubies and one pearl in a peece And

XVIII small buttons of golde with fower small pearles in a peece And fyve buttons of gold garnished with sparkes of diamonds Rubies and pearl in the feather." Stubbes had disapproved of extravagance and jaunty styling, but a hat of this richness was in the tradition of the jewel-embroidered *chaperons* of medieval monarchy. A hat sent for remodeling in 1602, when Elizabeth was 72, was both frivolous and grand. It was made from gold net and white tiffany, ruched with carnation silk and gleaming with 10 ounces of variegated spangles, and may have been a present.

Hoods, French hoods, cornets (caps), biliments (trimmings), crepins (rich jeweled hair nets), cauls and coifs were made for the Queen by her hoodmakers, Ellin Webbe, Charles Deberney and Margaret Sketts. Roger Mountague, a silkman, made cauls, crepins and riding shadows — wired enveloping hoods for protection against dust and sun while traveling. The Queen's ladies also made hoods.

It is not clear from the accounts where the responsibility for designing the clothes lay, but no doubt the Queen and her ladies passed ideas to the craftsmen, who in their turn contributed. There is here no suggestion that Raphael Hammond, the Queen's Capper and Hatter from the beginning of her reign to 1584, or his successor William Cooksbury, were 16th-century Ministres des Modes, foreshadowing Marie Antoinette's unfortunate intimacy with the couture. Only Miss Arnold's research has rescued them from oblivion and if the ladies followed the Queen's route to her milliner, they did it tactfully, perhaps buying gifts for the Queen.

This vivid and intimate glimpse into the wardrobe of a woman who deployed her femininity so successfully in a man's world, helps to place her own portraits and those of other ladies of the time in context. Hats are no longer just flat painted images, but beginning to take shape as millinery, three-dimensional real-life confections.

The seventeenth century

Above: James I of England by Paul de Critz, c1601. The king wears a hat in the most expensive and fashionable taste of his time, probably made from beaver-fur felt, with jeweled and feather trim.

The accession of James VI of Scotland to the English throne as James I did not curtail the brilliance that had marked the court of Elizabeth, but encouraged extravagance and ostentation throughout society. In Scotland he had been perennially poor, but once in England, James became almost spendthrift and his second order to the Royal Wardrobe was for hats. Whatever the reason — money, new status, or new fashions — its quantity and quality far exceeded any demand made by Queen Elizabeth.

In the light of imminent developments in North America (and Stubbes comments on their high cost) it is significant that James ordered 20 beaver hats. 17 of them were to be black, lined with taffeta, trimmed with black bands and feathers, perhaps for the period of court mourning; there was also a black riding hat, embroidered in gold and silver-trimmed with a white plume, and a gray one lined with green. Some may have been for the family. His wife, Anne of Denmark, was very fashion-conscious and a de Critz portrait shows her in hunting dress with a man-styled hat with chimney pot crown, and feather-trimmed with swooping brim. James was a doting father, and the hats ordered for his son James, in pink, purple, white and gray, embroidered with gold and silver, trimmed with multicolored feathers, as well as a cap like his father's, black trimmed with bird of paradise plumes, would have brought joy to the heart of any seven-year-old. To be a "beaver gallant" was the aim of every smart young man.

The last seven hats in the order were of ordinary felt, an economy, because beaver retailed at about 20 times the cost of other felts. An up-and-coming tradesman in William Fenner's *The Counter's Commonwealth* (1616) was advised: "Your four shilling Dutch felt shall be converted to a three pound beaver." 50 years later Samuel Pepys noted in his diary his qualms at ordering a beaver hat, and then worried about catching cold because it was too good to wear in the rain. This was a pity, because apart from fashion and prestige, both important to Samuel Pepys, the advantage of the beaver hat was that it was waterproof, if properly made, as well as light, a "Butterflys wing to put on" according to a character in *City Match* (1639). With long curling wigs coming into fashion during the 1650s, lightness was to be an important consideration to prevent the head becoming unbearably hot.

In North America, colonial rivalry intensified as beaver skins were recognized as a profitable export for which there was a steadily rising demand. Plymouth Plantation, the heartland of traditional North America, was, as early as 1620–21, assessed as a fur-trading post; the profits were scheduled to pay the development debt and the running costs until self-sufficiency was attained. The first year was bad; the cargo of skins, worth £300, was intercepted by the French, but when in 1631–32 William Bradford, Isaac Winslow and Miles Standish acted as undertakers and reorganized the trade, they exported 12,000 pounds of beaver, the pelts from about 6000 animals, which at between 14 and 20 shillings each, brought in £10,000 sterling. The establishment of the Hudson Bay Company in London in 1670 by Charles II, under Prince Rupert, 17 noblemen and gentry, illustrates the seriousness with which a rising mercantile nation considered the fur trade. The beaver played a most important part, leading to trade battles with the French in north Canada which were only resolved at the Treaty of Utrecht in 1713, when the territory ruled by France was ceded to Britain.

The sordid side of the trade we know only from Dutch records, though no doubt some of the practices were common whatever the nationality of the settler. In Fort Orange, later Albany, Adriaan van der Donck reported on the methods adopted by the settlers to undercut the Dutch East India Company, which held the monopoly on the product, and to defraud the Native Americans who brought skins to trade. They were waylaid by *Boschloopers* (bushrunners or brokers) before they entered the town, and within were tempted to "traffique" by independent "handelaers" eager to "adresse to speak to the wilden of trading." In payment, they were given trade goods, and gunpowder as well as liquor, which was recognized as irresponsible, if not dangerous, because its effects were incalculable. But, more valuable than fresh skins were the very coats from their backs in the trade "old coat," for "the coats which the Indians make of beaver skins and which they have for a long time around their bodies until the skins become foul with perspiration and grease are afterwards used by the hatters and make the best hats." Previously they had been dependent on old furs returned from Russia.

With increasing swiftness, the beaver retreated, their numbers diminished, and pelts rose ever higher in price.

The French were the first to go on record as making a conscious beaver substitute — demi castor. Their guild regulations were strict and mixing cheap with expensive fibers was specifically banned. An ingenious hatter devised a compromise, using beaver for the surface and cheaper hairs for the rest. It looked good and it cost less. Government reaction was extreme; in 1654 they risked a fine of 2000 livres, and, for a second offence death. Despite these draconian measures, trade flourished until in 1734, the regulations were rescinded. By that time the battle for demi castor was long since won. Many of the potentially offending hatters, those making for the provincial and the export trade in Normandy, were Huguenots and had emigrated to England and Germany after the Revocation of the Edict of Nantes in 1687, taking the technique with them; M. Mathieu is alleged by French historian Albert Franklin to have taught this valuable trade secret to English hatters, but since demi castors were known there from at least the 1650s, perhaps the exchange of expertise was earlier.

The fashionable shape for hats changed slowly but definitely during the first half of the 17th century. At the end of Elizabeth's reign they were high-crowned and had a broad brim. The shape is said to have relaxed during the Thirty Years' War (1618–48) which raged across Europe from Bohemia to Sweden and brought military styles into everyone's experience. High crowns, fashionable at the beginning of the period, with high pointed tops, dubbed Sugar Loaves or Steeples and which have acquired immortality as the prototype American Pilgrim

Above: A masculine-style hat worn for hunting by Anne of Denmark, painted by Paul de Critz, 1617. Anne's hat, probably of felt, has the carefully curved brim beginning to be fashionable; the crown is much higher than at the beginning of the century and has a rounded brim.

Above: The early 17th-century man's hat, as worn by the Gunpowder Plot conspirators in this print of 1605, was wide-brimmed; some had pointed sugar loaf crowns.

Below: A cavalier engraved by Abraham Bosse after Jean St. Igny, 1629 (from *Le Jardin de La Noblesse . . .*) wears the wide-brimmed plumed hat of the period.

hat, began to disappear as they were too difficult to keep on. As early as 1616, Bulwer had noted in *The Artificial Changeling*: "Every puff of wind deprived us of them, requiring the employment of one hand to keep them on."

But there were many styles, some worn by women as well as by men. According to another contemporary, Henry Peacham in *The Truth of Our Times* (1638), "There were those close to the head like barber's basons with narrow brims we were at the time beholden to the ladies of Spain for. After came up these with square crowns and brims almost as broad as a brewer's mash fat or a reasonable upper stone of a mustard quern."

Increasingly, low-crowned slouch hats were the norm, with floppy brims worn every which way, for there was no time to reblock or keep a hat in shape on campaign. It is these hats which have been identified with the royalist army fighting for King Charles I in the English Civil War of 1642 to 1645. The Parliamentary forces, by no means all short-cropped Roundheads, are usually identified with the hat with tapering flat-topped crown which was customary wear of the London citizenry and tradesmen class generally, the backbone of the Cromwellian forces, and which seems to have replaced the flat knitted cap by which they were known in the 16th century. As for decoration, identification took precedence at a time when military uniform was only just being introduced. Medieval troops had devices on their tunics, or distinctively colored hoods, but these were now replaced with, among other things, devices on hats. Soldiers on the King's side preferred red or pink hatbands and pink hat feathers, whereas Parliamentarians preferred orange feathers. On the other hand, either side might wear black or white! Less confusing, but perhaps difficult to see in the heat of battle, was the system of Field Marks which were chosen at the last moment. But it was difficult to find a distinguishing mark to tuck into a hatband that was both simple and unmistakable. At the battle of Marston Moor, for instance, the Parliament side wore white kerchiefs in their hats and all General Fairfax had to do when caught on the wrong side of the battle line was to take his white favor from his hat and, unmarked, ride through!

For active campaigning, there was that hardy perennial, the wooly hat. Francis

Wilson, fighting in the Low Countries in 1632, requested as well as warm waterproof clothes a "Monmouth cap to lye in my hutt in the night that I may serve my health." A useful importation from Spain where it was used for hunting was the Montero cap, which had peaks back and front which could be turned up, and earflaps.

For women, styles were more various. Englishwomen were noted for their dress consciousness and, as the Venetian ambassador wrote home in 1618:

> . . . dress so well . . . all ranks and condition of people being at liberty to invent new caprices. Thus, some wear on their heads worked bands with fine lace which, falling over their foreheads, form what our Venetian dames term "the mushrooms" on the temples. Others wear a large piece of work above the ear . . . others wear hats of various shapes; others wear a very small top knot. Some wear a moderate sized silk kerchief surmounted by a bit of crepe . . . Others have black velvet hoods turned over from the back of the neck to the forehead. Others wear embroidered caps, covering the whole head, while others . . . wear their . . . hair uncovered and curled.

He was describing the dress of the upper classes, which was at its most flamboyant at this period. At the end of Queen Elizabeth's reign, the women were no longer wearing the cone-shaped French farthingale, but barrel-shaped dresses and very wide high ruffs. The dress of the ordinary Englishwoman

Above: A felt hat of *c*1620 with the tapering crown with flat top and broad brim.

Below: Women wear regional caps with small pendant lappets, or enveloping hoods, and men broad-brimmed felt hats lower in the crown than those earlier in the century in this Netherlands street scene of 1652.

Above: Henrietta Maria, painted by Anthony van Dyck in 1632, wears an almost unisex broad-brimmed hat. Her semiformal dress has a masculine-style doublet bodice.

however, was still in the older style at this period, and a German traveler, Thomas Platter, had noticed Englishwomen wearing "high hats covered with velvet or silk" — in short the style which when exported to the American colonies became known as a Pilgrim hat. They remained in use by country-women and are shown in the invaluable series of etchings of Englishwomen and indeed women from all countries which were made by Wenceslaus Hollar in the 1630s and 1640s. Other hats in the series are sweeping masculine-style felts. For everyday occasions it seems to have been customary to wear a cap, sometimes with a hat on top, but hats alone were commonly worn for riding and Samuel Pepys, who preferred his women womanly, noted that "the sight did not please me," when in summer 1666, he saw "the Ladies of Honour dressed in their riding garbs . . . with periwigs and with hats, so that, only for a petticoat dragging under their man's coats, no one could take them for women in any way whatsoever."

More to his taste was his wife whom, in 1665, he had noted as "very fine in a new yellow birdseye hood, as the fashion is now." This style persisted for a long time, and simple silk hoods continued in use throughout most of the next century. They were made from lightweight silk, often black, and seem to have been a rectangular length of fabric shaped by gathering in at the crown of the head. They were draped neatly round the face and tied under the chin, and as such appear in the Hollar engravings. "So close, so very trim and neat/So round, so formal, so complete," as it is described in *Hudibras Redivivus* (1642).

Though they had their place in every woman's wardrobe, they were particularly associated with Nonconformists and Quakers, and are often referred to in American correspondence of the 17th and 18th centuries. They had a long and useful, if not very fashionable life, and as Mrs. Centilivre was to put it in *A Bold Stroke for a Wife* (1718): "Are the pinch'd cap and formal hood the emblems of sanctity? Does your virtue consist in your dress, Mrs. Prim?"

The caps had also been modified. They bore some resemblance to the embroidered Elizabethan coifs, but by the 1620s were generally made in plain linen, and had the front border turned back and trimmed with lace. Some may

Near right: An Englishwoman, engraved by Wenceslaus Hollar in 1640, wears a hat similar to that of Henrietta Maria.

Far right: A black hood as worn by *Autumn* in the series, *The Four Seasons*, engraved by Richard Geywood in 1654 from the Hollar original of 1644. This type of headdress was to continue in semi-fashionable use for at least a century.

Above left: An English
gentlewoman in winter dress,
an engraving by Wenceslaus,
1640, illustrates a back view of
a hood, from which it is
possible to see the gathering at
the nape of the neck.

Above right: An English
gentlewoman, engraved by
Wenceslaus Hollar, 1640, wears
a close-fitting white cap
trimmed with lace. It is the
beginning of a style which will
last into the next century.

Above: Women, especially
those from bourgeois
households, habitually wore
caps. They always had regional
characteristics and styles
similar to those worn in Jan
Steen's *Grace before Meat,*
*c*1660. There is an intriguing
resemblance to some in the
English 1560 group, *The*
Horsleydown Wedding. The
man, saying grace, has doffed
his indoor soft cap and holds it
in his hands.

Left: A peasant family by Le
Nain, mid-17th century. The
French headdress can be seen at
its most basic. Kerchiefs,
simple caps and broad-
brimmed felt hats were
common in most working
environments.

Right: An engraving of French gentlemen, *c*1655. The hats, worn straight, have low crowns and very slightly curving brims.

have been fastened under the chin, but it seems to have been more usual to draw them together under the hair at the back of the neck. Variations of this style, like the hood, were fashionable well into the 18th century.

In the last quarter of the century there were fundamental changes in the dress of both men and women. Since the mid-16th century, men had been wearing variations of the doublet and hose. The doublet had shortened by the beginning of James I's reign, and the breeches had become baggier, only to develop a more conventional body-shaped line in the reign of Charles I, best seen in the portraits of Van Dyck. In the 1650s and early 1660s, both had so loosened and shortened as to become frankly inconvenient. At the instigation of Charles II or Louis XIV, or both, according to the gossips, men began to wear a long straight coat over an inner coat or waistcoat and with simplified, knee-length breeches. It was a style which would in essentials continue through the late 17th to the 18th century and was the prototype of the three-piece suit as we know it today.

Women's fashions also moved on. Since the early 16th century they had worn dresses with a stiffened bodice, sometimes made separately from the skirt, as well as an overgown. Under the influence of the loose-fitting underdress or informal gowns which were being imported from the East in increasing numbers from the 1650s, they began to wear a manteau or slightly shaped overgown, relegating the boned bodice to undergarment or corset status, and the skirt to a semi-concealed petticoat.

But the key to the hat is the hairdressing, and for men this had not changed since the 1650s when they had begun to wear curled wigs, instead of the wispy long bobs which were the most that many men could manage with their natural attributes. Informally, the wig, which was expensive, as well as sometimes hot and uncomfortable, was replaced by a variety of soft caps, the shapes of which derived from those of the nightcaps worn at the beginning of the century. Often made from velvet, they could be quite imposing.

In the 1660s the hat, perched on the massy ridges of false curls, had a narrow brim and a shallow crown and was worn straight on the head. During the reign of Charles II, the brim grew wider and since it tended to droop if unsecured, cocking it, or turning it up, became the custom, and it was sometimes held in place with a loop and button. In 1667, with some disapproval, Pepys had noticed a "brisk young fellow with his hat cocked like a fool behind as the present fashion among the blades is." In a few more years it was to be known as the Monmouth cock called for the Duke of Monmouth, the natural son of Charles II and unsuccessful contender for the throne in 1689.

The wars of the Spanish succession from 1702 to 1714 familiarized and popularized military styling. There was the Ramillies cock, probably with the front of the brim turned up, which took its name from the battle of Ramillies in 1706 when the Duke of Marlborough routed the French and their allies. John Sly, the comic haberdasher featured by Addison in his satirical periodical *The Spectator*, has a keen eye for a topical twist of the brim. In no. 526 (1712) he is to note "the names of such country gentlemen as upon the approach of peace, have left the Hunting for the Military Cock of the hat." A little later in no. 532 (1713), he is broadening his scope and "preparing hats for several kinds of heads that make figures in the realms of Great Britain with cocks significant of their powers and faculties;" for lawyers and doctors they "do but just turn up to give a little life to their sagacity"; for the military man "they glare full in the face;" and "a familiar easy cock for all good companions between the above mentioned extremes." To these arrangements were added a plentiful trimming of gold lace and sometimes ostrich feathers.

But if men's hats modulated rather than changed style, this was not the case with women's headdress. From the 1640s their hair had been dressed in a coiffure low at the crown and wide at the sides. In the 1650s ringlets were replaced by side sweeps, which became a bush of curls in the 1660s. Very slowly the emphasis began to shift from width to height, and occasionally decoration began to appear at the crown of the head.

When the change finally came at the beginning of the 1680s, more or less coincidentally with the change to the loose manteau, it was so sudden that it was almost immediately personalized, and credited to the initiative of Marie Adelaide

Below left: A French couple of the 1670s from a Trachtenbuch. The woman wears a cap with a deep frill, and the man's hat has become wider, with the brim curved up decoratively. The man is wearing the type of dress which is to become current in the 18th century—a coat, waistcoat and breeches.

Below: a lady of the 1670s, by Paul Mignard, wears a lace cap with a double frill tied beneath the chin with a narrow black ribbon. There appears to be a lace veil pinned at the back.

de Scorailles de Roussillhe, Duchesse de Fontanges, young, pretty and in 1680, briefly, the reigning favorite of the French king Louis XIV. The Marquise de Maintenon was well placed to record the event, and wrote to a friend:

> At the chase one day, his nymph . . . had her knot of ribband caught and held by a branch; the royal lover . . . restore(d) the knot, and . . . offered it to his Amazon. Singular and sparkling although lacking in intelligence, she carried the knot of ribband to the top of her hair, and fixed it there with a long pin. Fortune willed that this coiffure without order or arrangement, suited her face . . . greatly. The King congratulate(d) her . . . the courtiers applauded . . .

This coiffure became the fashion of the day. All the ladies and the Queen herself found themselves obliged to adopt it.

It is conventional to refer to any headdress high at the brow as a fontange. It is a tribute to the influence of French fashion which was to dominate European style from the 17th to the mid-20th century, its prestige derived from the glamor of Versailles, the influence of Louis XIV and the shrewd calculation of chief minister Baptiste Colbert, who saw here a stimulus to French manufacturers and exports as well as the arts. Nevertheless, strictly speaking, the term is incorrect, and refers only to the striped ribbon bow.

From the late 1670s it was becoming fashionable to curl the hair at the forehead and pull the rest of the hair back in a knot, leaving the sides of the coiffure flat. Behind the curls, the frill of the cap grew higher, and the arrangement of cap or caps and frills more complex with terminology to suit. The best guide to the welter of Franglais fashion terms soon to be the mode is Mary Evelyn, daughter of diarist John Evelyn; a rhyming guide to international fashion speak was published by her father in 1690 as *Mundus Muliebris, or The Ladies Dressing Room Unlock'd*:

Below: The tall frills of the cap worn by the Lady of Quality in Winter Dress 1694, engraved by St. Jean, formed part of a complex accumulation of caps, bows and frills which began to be fashionable in the 1680s.

> Frelange, Fontange, Favourite,
> Monte la Haut, and Palisade,
> Sorti, Flandan (great helps to trade)
> Bourgoigne, Jardine, Cornett
> Frilal next upper Pinner set,
> Round which it does our Ladies please
> to spread the Hood call'd Rayonnes's:
>   . . .
>
> Where decent Veil was wont to hide,
> The Modest Sex Religious Pride:
> Let these yet prove too great a Load,
> Tis all compris'd in a Commode;
>   . . .
>
> Thus Face that e'rst near head was plac'd
> Imagine now about the Wast,
> For Tour on Tour and Tire on Tire,
> Like Steeple Bow on Grantham Spire . . .

The terms are defined in her *Fop Dictionary* which accompanies the poem. In alphabetical order:

> Bourgoigne. The first part of the Dress for the Head next the Hair. . . . Commode. a Frame of Wire, cover'd with Silk, on which the whole Head-Attire is adjusted at once upon a bust, or property of wood carved to the Breasts, like that which Perruque Makers set upon their Stalls. Cornet the upper Pinner dangling about the cheeks, like Hound Ears . . . Flandan. a Kind

of Pinner joyningd with the Bonnet. . . . Freland. Bonnet and Pinner together. Font-Ange the Top knot' so call'd from Mademoiselle de Fontange, one of the French King's Mistresses, who first wore it. . . . Jardinee. That single Pinner next the Bourgoigne. . . . Monte la Haut. Certaine degrees of Wire to raise the Dress. . . . Palisade. A Wire sustaining the Hair next to the Dutchess or first Knot. . . . Rayonee. Upper Hood, pinn'd in Circle like the Sunbeams. Sorti. a little knot of small Ribbon, peeping out between the Pinner and the Bonnet.

Above left and above: Lord and Lady Clapham dolls, 1695–1700, dressed in their clothes of the period. Lady Clapham's headdress has a tall frill behind which there is a silk-covered wire support; the fine fabric of the cap partially covers a ribbon-wrapped coil of hair.

It was as ephemeral as it was complicated. As a style it lasted many years, but there is only one example extant, worn by a doll, Lady Clapham, dating from about 1700 and now in the Victoria and Albert Museum. On her small wooden head can be seen the layers of caps, held together with handmade pins and supported on a frame of silk-covered wires. Her headdress has the gently rounded shape fashionable from about 1697 to 1700, after which it became much more angular and fan-shaped.

In about 1705 the headdress began to angle forwards and in 1710 it had begun to decline. Louis XIV is said to have disliked it and had ineffectually forbidden it to ladies as long ago as 1691. Nevertheless it remained in fashion at the French court until 1714 when Lady Sandwich, the wife of the English ambassador, is said to have appeared in an English-style low headdress, and the towering arrangements disappeared overnight as the court ladies followed a new idea.

There are only a few portraits to show the style, because it was a period in which, on the whole, the best portrait painters attempted to avoid the fashionable and thus give their clients, as well as themselves, the illusion of timeless immortality. But if not to be found in art, it does appear by courtesy of commerce. Fashion plates and illustrations make their first consistent appearance in this period and add greatly to our knowledge of the mode. They do not appear regularly until the second half of the 18th century, but they begin to add to the pictorial repertoire of the hat and the cap, and show the milliner's ideal rather than the reality.

THE BEAVER

The animal whose fur has for centuries been used for making felt hats is a bulky rodent which, when fully grown, reaches thirty inches long plus a twelve-inch tail, and weighs about 50 lbs. Its body is thickly covered with soft brown fur; it has short legs, the hind legs being webbed, and the conspicuous tail is flat and covered with scaly hairless skin. With these webbed hind legs and flat tail and its ability to close its nostrils under water, it is a powerful swimmer and diver.

The beaver has been extinct in England since the 9th century, though the presence of many place names commencing with beaver or Bever indicates it was a well-known creature in river valleys at one time. In Scotland there are records of the beaver being seen until some time in the 16th century.

The *Castor fiber*, or European beaver, is found in the Rhône valley in France, in north Europe in Poland and in Norway, as well as parts of northern Asia and Siberia. It lives in burrows but feeds on aquatic roots as well as the bark of trees. *Castor canadensis*, the Canadian or American beaver, lives in the sub-arctic regions and makes lodges of logs and mud which it constructs across streams and in lakes. Though it accumulates food in the summer and spends most of the winter sleeping, it does not hibernate even in the most frosty weather.

The nature of many animal furs, including that of the beaver, the nutria or coypu, the hare and even the rabbit, all used for felt, is such that the fibers, once removed from the skin, cling in a particular form due to their notched or ragged edges, invariably all pointing in one direction. Though not visible to the naked eye, the microscope reveals this structure readily. With the beaver, the fibers or beaver-down as they are called, are thicker and softer than in other animals, and so can give a finer felt; at the same time the hairs vary in size according to whether they are inner or outer, and in preparing the first the longer guard hairs are removed. It is the under fur which is used for the felt.

With the dangers of overhunting of the beaver, especially in North America, and restrictions on their being killed, the use of fur from the coypu, the rabbit and the hare has very much taken over. The fur of nondomesticated animals is superior to that from those bred for the purpose.

The beaver's other claim to fame in the world of natural history is in its engineering feats; making log dams by cutting the timber with its teeth, pushing them downstream into position and plastering them with mud with its forefeet. Their dams defy the strongest currents and are often a hundred feet wide.

With the great reduction today in the use of beaver fur for hat-making, it seems that the beaver will live on as dam-builders, rather than die out as hat providers.

The eighteenth century

During the 18th century, hats as we know them today entered the fashionable wardrobe. At the beginning of the century, women were wearing almost recognizable descendants of the 16th-century coif, at its end Caps of Liberty and smart hats as ephemeral as the gossip which inspired them, while men lost the peacock role and began to wear the plain black hat, variations of which are still with us.

For the early part of the period, a woman's daily dress always included a cap, which in shape still retained traces of its 16th-century origins. Made from plain white linen, it now consisted of a caul, a rounded panel covering the back of the head, extended to the front with a band usually finished with a trimming, either lace or a frill.

The styles of 1725 and 1726, formal and informal, are comprehensively illustrated in miniature by the painter and illustrator Bernard Lens. His set of drawings, *The Exact Dress of the Head drawn from the Life at Court, Opera, Theatre park &c.. from the Quality and Gentry of ye British Nation*, includes 81 women and 12 men wearing headcoverings which are still recognizable descendants of those fashionable at the beginning of the century, though the high front frill is now

Below left: Ladies' caps drawn by Bernard Lens in 1725–26. Made from lace, they fitted the crown of the head and have pendant lappets which suggests that they are for formal wear. Informally they can be folded over the cap.

Below: A young man wearing a small three-cornered hat from a series drawn by Bernard Lens, 1725–26. The loops are part-decorative and part-functional and help to hold the brim in the correct arrangement.

little more than a tiny scallop and the large men's hats are now small, neat and three-cornered, and worn over neat tied-back wigs. Despite the limits of the style, there is great variety of effect. Informally, caps can be enveloping with long side panels, but for dress occasions sometimes little more than crown and frill and worn perched on the top of the head, and called pinners because of their means of attachment. Lappets are now mainly for formal and court wear. By the 1740s they had diminished to a mere rosette or pom pom.

Although almost every woman wore caps, almost none survive though there are many of the expensive lace trimmings, the cap crowns and the lappets. Whereas most ladies would have worn just a simple lace trimming of indeterminate origin, the most expensive were made from French or Flemish lace. At the French court, etiquette and taste scheduled needlepoint lace, such as Venetian or *point de Venise* for formal wear in winter, and in summer, the lighter, more supple bobbin laces. As dress style became more bouffant and less rigid, the French laces of Alençon and Argentan competed with Flemish lace from Brussels (called *point d'Angleterre* for commercial reasons), Mechlin, Binche and Chantilly.

The arrangement of the frill harmonized with the line of the dress. That of the 1720s, for instance, still retained a central "kick" reminiscent of the high headdresses at the beginning of the century. In the 1730s it was evenly arranged, rounded like the skirts, and in the 1740s and 1750s began to spread laterally, sometimes reinforced with wire. One version was called the Butterfly and the line followed that of the side hoops at their widest in the 1740s. In the 1760s, the hair began to be dressed higher at the forehead, and it was then that the cap seems to have become dispensable.

The hat was widely worn, placed over the cap in the early part of the century. It had a low crown and a wide brim. It was among the stock in trade of milliners who according to R. Campbell's *The London Tradesman* (1745), sold light accessories as well as "Hats Hoods and Caps of all sorts of materials . . . in short they furnish everything to the Ladies, that can contribute to set off their Beauty, increase their Vanity or render them ridiculous." They needed to be good needlewomen as well as "Perfect Connoisseur[s] in Dress and Fashion." This, he writes, comes from Paris where some kept Agents "who have nothing else to do but watch the Motions of the Fashion and procure Intelligence of the Changes which she signifies to her Principals, with as much Zeal and Secrecy as an

Right: A lady's hat, *c*1760, from the Rougemont House Costume Museum, Exeter. It is made from velum sandwiched between two layers of silk and stamped with a lace-like design. The trimming of cotton net and ribbon may no longer be in its original arrangement.

Left: *The Review*, a satirical engraving of 1745, illustrates typical Londoners; the women wear broad-brimmed hats with both pointed and flat crowns over their caps, rivalling in size their wide side hoops. The men's hats are cocked in different ways, and in the foreground a man wears a country-style hat with turned-up brim.

Ambassador of the Plenipotentiary would the important Discovery of some political intrigue." Despite "vast profits," they paid their workwomen so poorly that the constant pressure to be polite in the presence of the smart world made them easy victims for the young men-about-town.

But although many hats were worn, few survive. Not all were as recherché as those made by Campbell's upmarket milliners. An advertisement in the *Salisbury Journal* (1756) notes: "Horsehair hats, womens size 9/- [shillings] a dozen Paper hats 1/5 –3/- a dozen." This was possibly an export and wholesale range, for Harriot Paine was selling in Boston, Massachusetts, in 1751 and 1753 "Saxon blue silk and Hair hatts, black horsehair and leghorn bonnet, embossed and stampt Sattin hatts" as well as "Fine beverett hats with tabby linings." A hat in the collection of the Victoria and Albert Museum suggests that the crinoline was a woven mixture of silk and horsehair giving a light flexible texture. A surviving paper hat shows it to have been made of good, soft card impressed with a lace design, and it somewhat resembles a cake doily as we know it today. Very popular was chip made from woven willow shavings and most popular of all straw. The latter two were often covered or faced with silk.

Engravings and portraits show the hats echoing the line of the dresses, having medium-width brims and crowns in the 1720s and 1730s, very wide and floppy in the 1740s, some having deep scalloped brims and others a small pointed crown which may be a recollection of the styling which still persisted in the country from the early 17th century. In the 1750s and 1760s they become smaller. The trimmings were many and various, ribbon, flowers, passementerie and lace, and were mostly concentrated around the junction of crown and brim and at the edge. Newspapers, both English and American, give the names of the styles; Kitty Fisher and Garrick bonnets suggest that the stage was one inspiration, society another (Ranalegh bonnets and Queens bonnets) and even politics (Russian, French and Quebec bonnets), but in the absence of pictures, their particular qualities are lost to us.

A basic material of the trade as it had been from early times was straw, though it had been mainly used in a workaday utilitarian context. Mrs. Pepys had tried on a straw hat during a visit to the country in the summer of 1667 and, as Mr. Pepys noted, "it did become (her) mightily." By the 18th century they were becoming sophisticated town fashion. Charles de Saussure, a Swiss traveler, noted in 1727 "small hats of straw that are vastly becoming. Ladies even of the

Below: Mary Countess Howe, for her portrait by Thomas Gainsborough about 1765, wears a ribbon-trimmed hat at a straight—almost Chinese—angle over a light, indoor cap.

Above: Peter Perez Burdett and his first wife, Hannah, in 1765, by Joseph Wright of Derby. She wears a broad-brimmed straw, he a three-cornered hat tilted back.

highest rank are thus attired when they go walking or make a simple visit."

Basic straw hats were locally made, and it has been suggested that the craft came to England from Liège in Belgium from where there was a migration of craftsmen in the early 16th century. The highest quality straws came from Leghorn in Italy, where soil and climatic conditions gave a wheat straw which had the requisite length, fineness and flexibility. It was a well-established industry and Thomas Coryate had noted in his *Crudities* (1611): "most delicate strawen hats, which both men and women use in most places in that Province, but especially the women. For those that the women wear are very pretty, some of them having at least a hundred seames made with silk." From Leghorn the craft moved south to Florence and north over the Alps to Switzerland.

With increasing demand, the English industry also expanded, especially in the Midlands and in Bedfordshire and Hertfordshire to the north of London. They were probably catering for the basic end of the market, and by 1689 were well enough established to petition the government against an attempt by the hatters to increase the trade in felt hats; by 1719 they were sufficiently confident of their quality to protest against the import of chip plait from the Netherlands and Leghorn straw.

The English export trade in hats to the American colonies was very profitable.

It was also resented by the Americans as their own taste, skill and expertise developed; the material, wheat and plant straw, was ubiquitous and the difference in cost between material and finished product seemed excessive. No doubt many attempts were made to make an acceptable and fashionable local product, but most foundered on the problem of finding a straw as well adapted as the Leghorn and in getting the correct weave in the braid. The unique quality of a Leghorn was its smoothness. While the English braids were stitched and overlapped, leaving ridges, the Leghorn plaits were so made that they could be laid edge to edge.

By the 1790s, the problem of obtaining fashionable hats had become acute. The United States was independent of England and the Revolutionary wars were interrupting supplies from Europe. Also straw hats and bonnets were high fashion. A girl of 12, Betsy Metcalfe of Providence, Rhode Island, was to launch the American millinery industry on its way.

The first bonnet she made in 1798 is said to be still in the collection of the Rhode Island Literary and Historical Society. It was made from homegrown oat straw which she smoothed with her scissors and split with her thumbnail. She had never braided straw, but advised by an aunt, who seems to have known something of the technique, she went from six to seven straw braid, "and then it was right." It was "smoothed with a junk bottle" and made up. With bobbin lace inserted like openwork, bleached in sulfur fumes, presumably finished and blocked, and lined with pink, it was much admired, and orders from friends flowed in.

American initiative did not stop here and in the early 19th century, when there was a continuing problem finding substitutes for Leghorn straw, American women were in the forefront of finding plant substitutes for expensive Italian imports. The quest was steadily encouraged by the English Royal Society of Arts, and Sybilla Masters of Philadelphia and Sophia Woodhouse from Connecticut in 1821 both won prizes for finding practical alternatives.

Hats and bonnets were already reaching the heights of fashion in the 1760s. The line of the dress was beginning to change, the point of emphasis moving upwards as the waist and then the level of the coiffure rose. In the last quarter of the 18th century, Paris fashion became definitive and the envy of the women of the civilized world.

A coincidence happy for *les modes*, if profoundly unfortunate for a nation, brought a dress-conscious extravagant young girl, Marie Antoinette, to the throne of France in 1773 and provided her with a collaborator, Rose Bertin, derisively called her *Ministre de Modes*, who was as inspired as a designer as she appeared to be at publicity and attracting notoriety. It makes her a credible founding mother of the couture profession. She was a milliner and is known to us only through contemporary gossip, account books and bills, part of the Doucet collection in the University of Paris as well as lawsuits, for the hats, caps and all but one of the dresses which she trimmed with a multitude of precious and fragile nonsenses have disappeared. There are fashion plates in plenty at this period in the *Galerie des Modes* and the *Journal des Modes*, but it was not then the custom to give commercial credits. In any case, Rose Bertin's clientele would have been offended at such contact with commerce, and expected a unique creation for the price and no extra facilities for copyists.

Rose Bertin was born in Abbeville in 1747, trained as a milliner's apprentice and by 1772, having opened her own establishment, Le Grand Moghul, in the rue Saint Honoré, had been introduced to the then Dauphine, Marie Antoinette, by her hairdresser, Leonard. She attracted attention with her designs and a mixture of cheek and charm not appreciated by colleagues or the more old-fashioned of

Above: Rose Bertin (1744–1813), the first milliner or *marchande des modes* to achieve international fame.

the nobility. To Beaulieu, her rival, "She had the airs of a Duchess and was not even a bourgeoise" and to Madame de Oberkirch, who left the salon without buying, "her chatter is amusing . . . a mixture of hauteur and baseness which bordered on impertinence. The Queen . . . allowed her a familiarity of which she took advantage." Unfortunately, no rival or client has left a description of the salon, though it must have been seemly and luxurious. Soon the names of the crowned heads and the nobility of Europe are to be found in her account books. The Czarina and her ladies were enthusiastic customers, as well as the English nobility, though not the royal family. As a member, indeed eventually Mistress of the *Marchande des Modes*, which became an independent corporation in 1776, she should have made only coiffures, hats and bonnets and trimmings for dresses, but her scope seems to have extended more widely, no doubt under an informal system of subcontracting. The Poufs or caps that she concocted and the hats were poised on coiffures which by the 1770s were reaching the summit of an ascent begun in the 1760s. An amazing altitude is a feature of the fashion plates, but analysis of portraits suggests that this is a graphic convention to stress the fashionable obsession and also to give room for the detail of the trimming which was loaded on the head. In fact, even at its highest, the dressed hair never rose further above the crown than the distance between eyes and chin. With a close, competitive and bored high society under constant challenge from an increasingly ambitious bourgeoisie, the key to success in the millinery business was novelty and topicality. Charming as they were, the ingenious novelties she balanced on the head were only miniatures.

Nevertheless the detail was well reported. In 1774, Louis XVI was inoculated

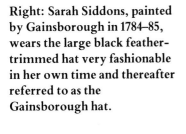

Right: Sarah Siddons, painted by Gainsborough in 1784–85, wears the large black feather-trimmed hat very fashionable in her own time and thereafter referred to as the Gainsborough hat.

against smallpox, an event which Bertin commemorated in the Pouf à l'Innocula-tion, which included a rising sun, to illustrate the king's descent from Le Roi Soleil, Louis XIV, an olive tree around which coiled a snake representing the Greek god of healing, Aesculapius, together with a hammer to symbolize victory over disease. Beaulard, Bertin's rival milliner, introduced the Pouf à la Circonst-ances and the Pouf aux Sentiments, loaded with miniatures of whatever the wearer held dear. Well known is the headdress on which is a vessel in full sail, commemorating the ship *La Belle Poule*. Hats and capes were also named after newsworthy events such as the first balloon ascents, so much a feature of the decade. In America there was a hat called a Hot Air Balloon, in France in 1784 a bonnet à la Montgolfier and in England a Lundardi hat and a Balloon bonnet. This fashion, however, seems to have floated downmarket quite quickly and is said to be the type of black silk hat with soft crown and caplike brim which had become general wear in the English countryside by the 1780s and is worn by the women in George Stubbs' paintings of *The Harvesters* (1785) and *The Reapers*.

Much of what Bertin made was, of course, less newsworthy. For Madame du Barry, favorite of the late king Louis XV, she made several hats in 1779, a large white straw with brim turned up on both sides, trimmed with ribbon, blue with black spots and a plume. Straw must have been an all-weather fabric for in January 1780, she made another in white, faced with brown silk and trimmed with a large feather panache. She also remodeled hats for her clients.

But fashion was by no means exclusively French. The wife of President John Adams described her daughter Abigail in full formal dress in 1786 as wearing a gown and petticoat of red-and-white striped gauze and with it a small white

Left: Semi-formal dress from the *Galerie des Modes*, 1779. The lady wears a cap crowned with feathers, the man a compromise between the round and the three-cornered hat.

Right: A satirical view of the fashions of 1780, a mezzotint by Carrington Bowles. The ladies' hats and caps are exaggeratedly large, and there is a good view of the Calache hood. The young sportsman has his hat pulled into a three-cornered shape with decorative gold cords.

leghorn bonnet bound with pink satin ribbon, turned up at the side with a steel buckle and band confining a large pink bow: there was a large bow of the same pink ribbon behind, a wreath of full-blown roses around the crown and another of buds at the side of the hat, which "being placed at the back of the hair brought the roses to the edge. You see it clearly?" writes her mother.

Bertin and Paris fashion survived the French Revolution and all the dislocation in the luxury trades. She continued to supply a diminishing supply of accessories to Marie Antoinette in the Temple until her execution. She also made Tricoleur cockades. As business diminished and her clientele either literally lost their heads or emigrated, she went on a series of foreign tours visiting England and the rest of Europe, in part selling and in part trying to collect old debts. She returned to Paris permanently in 1810, and died at her country home in Epinay-sur-Seine, so it is said, respected by the poor and all who knew her.

As rare as the elaborate concoctions of high fashion are the simple fitted caps which most women wore within the house. Made from muslin or silk gauze and variously trimmed, usually with lace and ribbon, they were often homemade.

For a brief period in the 1780s and 1790s in France, they were topically replaced with a simple triangular kerchief, draped *à la Paysanne*.

A new type of hood, the Calache, or calash, was introduced in 1772. Lightweight and stiffened with cane or whalebone, it was an updated version of the bongrace of Tudor times. As described by *The London Magazine* in 1772 it was so constructed "as with a ribbon pulled it can entirely cover the face by which means it is preserved from the sun. It serves instead of a hat and does not require the hair to be dressed. It is usually worn for walking parties." Initially informal, it was also useful to protect the more elaborate and fragile type of millinery and was to have a long life. Revived in the 1830s, it disappeared finally in the 1850s.

Men's hat styling moved in the opposite direction to that of the ladies; during the 18th century, from elaborate and ostentatious, it became plain. At the beginning of the period, the cocked hat was the norm. The War of the Spanish Succession was involving most of Europe and military styles were popular. The Seven Years' War (1756–1763) confirmed the vogue. One style named after Austrian Field-Marshal Baptiste Leonard von Khevenhüller with the front brim cocked up, shaped with a pinch in the front and the back arranged in two small points was extremely popular with both military and naval men. In 1754, an attempt to standardize military headgear in England had the perverse effect of stimulating each colonel to a desperate search for something unique and smart for his particular troop: convenience was not a criterion. The arrangement of the cocks had however initially been designed to help shed the rain from the brim. The French term for the points, *gouttières*, or gutters, recalls this usage.

As important as the shape of the hat was the way it was worn. In Mrs.

Above: A satirical view of the purchase of a new semiformal cap or pouf in the 1780s. It was usual for a milliner to visit a good customer. In addition to making hats and caps they also dealt in lace and trimmings.

Left: Sally Sandford Perrit painted by R. Moulthrop in 1790. She wears a pouf of ruched gauze and ribbons and a fashionable compromise between cap and headdress.

Right: The Pantheon Macaroni, *c***1775. His exaggeratedly smart outfit includes a very small hat perched on his excessively tall wig.**

Far right: A fashionable man engraved by Defraine, 1784. He wears a hat turned up at back and front giving it a point at each side, said to have been called a "L'Androsmane."

Centilivre's play, *The Stolen Heiress* (1714), we are told: "Your beaux wear their hat thus (putting it under his arm), your conceited wits thus (putting it over his left eye); your country squire thus (putting it behind his wig)." In Thomas Gainsborough's portrait of country gentleman Mr. Andrews with his wife, seated in a landscape, he does indeed wear his hat in exactly this way.

Within this general shape, the hat balanced the male silhouette and almost seemed to act as a counterpoise to the spread of the skirts of the coat. Thus hats were large until the 1720s when coats were comparatively wide, and loose, wide but neat in the 1740s when coats flared at the hem, and began to get smaller in the 1760s when the suit was cut closer to the figure. For wear in the house, and when the wig was thankfully discarded, there were soft rich colored caps, almost turban size, for the flowing undress gowns or banyans.

The shape was becoming regularized, but the niceties of arrangement and angle were crucial to the fashionable. In 1762, the *London Chronicle* gave an ironical account of the subtleties in the arrangement of a hat with a brim: "on average 6 inches and three-fifths broad . . . cocked between a Quaker and a Khevenhüller . . . open before, like a church-spout, or the tin scales they weigh flour in; some . . . sharper like the nose of a greyhound."

As for the angle: "the beaux of Moorfields Mall (city tradesmen) wear theirs diagonally over their left or right eye; . . . some wear their hats (with the corners which should come over their forehead in a direct line) pointed into the air: those are the Gawkies; others do not half cover their heads."

As for trimmings, Quakers did not wear any, and let the hat flap and "the hat edged with a gold binding belongs to the brothers of the turf."

The ultra-smart beaux of the 1770s, satirized as Macaronies because of their undue fondness for foreign fashions, wore short skintight clothes and tiny neatly cocked hats perched on their towering wigs. The song popular at the time of the American Revolutionary war about Yankee Doodle who "stuck a feather in his cap and called it Macaroni" will recall their eccentricities for all time. Very popular at this period was the Nivernois hat, neat and small with brim cocked into three equidistant points, called after the Duke de Nivernois, French ambassador to England between 1761 and 1762. By the end of the century,

Left: *The Reapers* by J. Stubbs, 1785. This is a rather idealized view of harvesters but shows the typical country clothes. The woman wears a light black hat large enough to serve as a sunbonnet and with some pretensions to fashion. The horseman wears a broad-brimmed felt, similar but less battered than that of the field worker.

Below: The Wedgwood family by J. Stubbs, *c*1780. They are wearing upmarket English country styling, and the ladies' hats bear comparison with that worn by Sarah Siddons, though they have a slightly more tailored look. The equestrienne wears a pretty feminine hat with her masculine-styled clothing, an unusual compromise for the period when cross-dressing for sport was the norm.

especially by the more formal, the popular hat was called the l'Androsmane in France and the Continental in America. In this the front and the back brim were so folded that there were but two points, one at each side. In the way that the three-cornered hat became the Tricorne of the 19th century, so this was termed the Bicorne. It has been suggested that this shape was adopted by the Incroyables, the nouveaux riches young survivors of post-Revolutionary France, because it was a compromise, committing them neither to the Tricorne of the ancien régime, nor to the "pot hat" of the Republicans.

By the third quarter of the century it had been realized that wearing hats as well as wigs was hot, especially in fine weather. With the practice of doffing the hat as a courtesy in greeting and not wearing it in the presence of a superior, in any case hats frequently spent more time under the arm than on the head. For formal occasions, the Chapeau Bras was introduced. It was made flat and light and the crown was not deep enough to wear. However, it could still pose a problem for the owner. In 1774, *The London Magazine* gently mocked the country boor who "sometimes has it in his hand, sometimes in his mouth and often betrayed an inclination to put it on his head, concluding that it was a damned troublesome useless thing."

There was an alternative to the cocked hat, the round hat. This had been a basic country style at the beginning of the century, worn for its practicality. With an increased appreciation of what the upper classes and philosophers saw as the advantages of country living, it began to enter the fashionable town wardrobe. For traveling and informal wear it had advantages; it was easy to keep on; it shaded the eyes and the neck; if sufficiently hard it protected the head from overhanging branches.

The first American fashion to reach the world wardrobe, it was also the hat of the radical revolutionary. It seems to have arrived in the chic masculine wardrobe by way of France, which had obtained it from America, where an old-style Quaker hat was in fairly common use. It had been popularized there by Benjamin Franklin and General Lafayette, the architects of the Franco-American alliance during the Revolutionary wars. In England it was particularly popular with the Whigs, the supporters of American independence, and was worn, for instance, by Charles James Fox. It was usually black, but fawn and gray were popular in the summer.

Sports hats were beginning to feature in the 18th century. They were to a great extent unisex and women wore the jockey-type hunting cap, sometimes padded, or the neat three-cornered hat and the round hat with their masculine-styled riding coats.

For France the years 1789–94 were those of Revolution and at the height of the Terror, all these types of hat were supplanted for a brief period by the Red Cap of Liberty. It had been the symbol of the Jacobin and the Cordelier Clubs, and of the extreme republican group, the Sansculottes. A scarlet stocking cap, it was said to represent the pileus, the cap which had symbolized the rights of a free citizen in Ancient Rome. According to the author of *De l'origine de la forme du bonnet de la liberté* (1796), red was the color of blood shed in the cause of the revolution. It was in great evidence at the *Fête de la Federation* and appeared on many of the commemoration pieces. Robespierre, however, blocked an attempt to make it universal and compulsory in 1792. The red, white and blue cockade, the invention of Lafayette, was thought sufficient and more suitable for conveying a national unity rather than an extremism that went beyond law. Moreover there was disquiet about its validity for wear by women, since it implied an acceptance of their political responsibility.

For most men's hats or masculine-style hats, the basic material was felt.

Left: A political caricature from 1774. Macaroni-making in Boston focuses on American resentment at British restraints on their trade, including tea and hats. The hats of the colonists are broad-brimmed and uncocked, country and colonial styles which became high fashion in the 19th century. Note also the revolutionary cockade.

Encyclopedias were a feature of the enlightenment and in the *Encyclopédie de Sciences* (1752–1772) and its successor, the *Encyclopédie méthodique* (1787), there are very detailed accounts of the making of the felt hat. It brings into focus a process which has been only known from guild ordinances and the basic practice in primitive communities. Despite the hard work and the constant alternations between heat and cold necessary to break down and bond the fibers and shape the hats, hatters and feltmakers before the 18th century seem to have been healthy and prosperous. Queen Elizabeth, saluted by loyal hatters on the way to Tilbury, is said to have been so impressed with their appearance that she thought they were gentlemen; and afterwards this was always the way in which they referred to themselves: Gentlemen Hatters.

According to Campbell, hat-making was a good if dirty trade. Many of the workshops were small, little more than cottage outhouses, but larger workshops were being established to cope with home demand and in particular for the export trade. In England the trade began to coalesce; in London, in Southwark south of the River Thames, the traditional base for the London hatters; in the West Country, where wool was good and convenient for export from the port of Bristol; in Lancashire near Manchester where Stockport has remained the main center for the trade today. The advantages here were said to be good coal for fuel and clean water. It was also near to the port of Liverpool. In France, the best hats

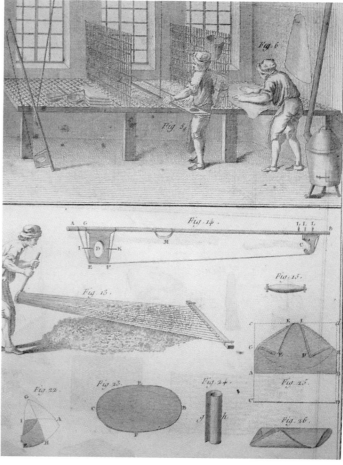

Above: The products of the boursier or pursemaker, from Panckoucke's *Encyclopédie*, also included men's and children's informal and protective caps as well as military headgear.

Above right: An illustration showing the making of felt hats from Panckoucke. The hairs are prepared and the fibers are bowed to ensure their correct alignment and worked to form. The pattern may be seen pinned to the wall. The bow is marked Fig. 14.

were made in Paris, where the Corporations tried to exercise quality control over the national output and there were further centers in Normandy and near Marseilles.

Both countries tried to protect their own product by imposing high tariffs on imports, and consequently smuggling was as widespread as legitimate trade. They had designs on the Spanish and Portuguese market, Italy, Germany and of course the Americas and the West Indies. An unbiased Belgian assessment of their respective qualities published in the *Almanach des négociants* (1762), gives Paris the superiority: the countries are the equal in finish and style, but Paris is more skilful in its use of beaver, its dyeing and its low price, a quarter that of London.

In no sense were the American colonists passive recipients of costly imported hats; after all, they were surrounded by choice raw material and there were expert hatmakers among them. Moreover they were closer to the important export markets of South America and the West Indies. A flourishing if small-scale industry was quick to develop. In 1731, the English feltmakers attempted to end this threatening competition by persuading Parliament to pass the Hat Act, prohibiting the Americans from exporting, and even attempting to control American home production.

By 1780, after Independence, Zadoc Benedict established the first felt hat factory at Danbury, Connecticut, which is said to have made 18 felt hats a week. This should however be seen in context. An inventory of a London hatter in a moderately sized business, made by Margaret Barwise of Southwark, in 1765, notes that in the course of routine trade she had 132 hats in stock, the best of which were worth 15/- [shillings], the wages of one of her workers. She did not make the best quality hats for, like most London hat-makers she used not beaver

Left: The felt shapes are being formed, strengthened and shrunk using heat, water and manipulation. The plank or trough changes little over the years. The blocks for the final shaping of the hats can be seen stacked on the shelf and the oven where the hats are drying.

but a mixture of wool and rabbit fur. But the Americans were quick to catch up and by 1800, when Philadelphia had become the main center of production, it was valued at the equivalent of one million dollars yearly.

The process of converting hair and wool into felt and then into bats which were shrunk and then blocked into shape as hats was one which on a large scale required organization and teamwork, and was similar in England and France. The journeymen hatters as they were called were well paid, proud of their craft and tightly organized with long-established customs to safeguard themselves against their employers. Both employment and allocation of work were controled to a large extent by the workers, and safeguarded by a complicated system of fines, mostly paid out in beer.

It is surprising that they were as healthy as they claimed to be, because from mid-18th century, they were using a mixture of a mercury solution and nitric acid to soften the hair so that it could be felted, a process which, from the shade that it turned the pelt, was known as Carroting to the English and *Rougit* to the French. This *Eau de composition* or *Secrets* as they were known colloquially, the Abbé Nollet writes in his definitive account of the trade in 1765, was an English process brought back by a French hat-maker returned from England. Released by the heat and warmth of the felting and blocking process, the mercury fumes were extremely dangerous. By the end of the 18th century, it was only too easy to suffer from hatters' shakes, and mad hatters were noticed by the medical profession as well as by Lewis Carroll as late as the 1860s, even if they never found their way into the texts on the craft of hat-making. Nevertheless, this phenomenon must have been an unstated stimulus in the progress towards mechanization which was to be the story of the hat-maker in the 19th century.

Hat-making is best told in pictures and these have been taken from the *Encyclopédie Méthodique* (1786). The comment is by Dorothy Richardson, a Yorkshire rector's daughter traveling in Lancashire in 1778. She is describing the process at Bent Hall, the factory owned by Andrew Clegg in Oldham. He had founded it in 1748 and she is amazed that it is so large he spends £100 annually on packing paper alone. It is the earliest description of an English hat factory and tallies completely with the French process. This account is taken from her unpublished travel diary, in the John Rylands Library, University of Manchester. Staying with the Clegg family, their house and factory set in woods and green fields in what is now a sooty conurbation, she goes to see the factory, a "very large pile of buildings":

I was present at the whole process of making a hat, and I am surpris'd how a low priz'd one can be afforded it goes thro' such a number of hands. 1st the weighing the Beaver, down, wool etc which is done for every hat separately . . . 2nd the bowing, the different materials are mix'd together and laid upon a flat table with long chinks cut through to let out the dust, upon this they have a bow resembling that belonging to a violin but larger whose string is worked by a little bow stick and thus made to play upon the furs, til they are mix'd in the nicest manner and form two gores of an oval form ending in an acute angle at the top; this is the most difficult operation as it requires great justness of the hand, to make the stuff fall together, so that it may be everywhere the same thickness, with what stuff remains they strengthen the thin places and designedly make them the thickest in the brim near the Crown. The gores thus finished are hardened into closer flakes by pressing a piece of leather call'd a hardening skin upon them and then 3rd they are carried to the Bason a sort of bench with an iron plate fix'd in it, under which is a little fire; one of the hardening gores sprinkled with water, is laid upon the plate, a sort of mould is laid upon it and the heat of the fire with the pressing imbody the stuff into a slight hairy felt; after which turning up the edges all round, over the mould, they lay it by and proceed in the same manner with the other Gore. When finished the two are joined together so as to meet in an angle at the top and form one conical cap. The hat thus basond is 4th remov'd to a kind of trough resembling a Mill Hopper, going sloping down from the edge to the bottom, which is a Copper Kettle fill'd with hotwater & grounds; on the sloping side, call'd the plank, the bason'd Hat is laid, being first dipt in the kettle & here they work it, by rolling & unrolling it again and again, one part after another first with the hand & then with a little wooden roller: taking care to dip it from time to time; till at length by thus thickening it it is reduced to the dimension of the intended Hat. 5th They proceed to give the hat its proper form which is done by laying the conical cap on a wooden block of the intended size of the crown of a Hat & tying it round with a pack thread call'd a Commander after which with a piece of iron or copper bent to the purpose & called a stamper they gradually drive down the Commander all around, till it has reach'd the bottom of the block & thus the Crown is formed; what remains below the string being the brim. The Hat now being set to dry they 6th singe it, then it is pounced or rubb'd over with pumice to take off the coarse nap, then rubb'd with sealskin to lay the nap still finer & lastly carded with a fine card-7th The Hatt is set upon its block tied about with pack thread to be dyed: the copper usually holds 10 and 12 dozen of Hats; the dye is made of logwood, verdigrease, copperas & elder bark to which some add brazilleto, galls and sumac. Here the hat is kept boiling for about three quarters of an hour, then taken out & set to cool, then return'd to the dye & this is repeated ten or twelve times-7th [sic] the Hat is then dried in a stove, which is so hot I could but stay in it a moment, it is circular has shelves from top to bottom upon which the hats were laid — when dry the Hat then is stif'ned then beaten over with a brush & last rubb'd with the hand. It is 9th put on the steaming Bason which is a little Hearth cover'd with an iron plate on this is laid cloths sprinkled with water to prevent the Hat from burning & the Hat is placed upon them, the brim downwards; when moderately hot the workman strikes gently on the brim with the flat of his hand to incorporate the joinings, turning it backwards & forwards and at last setting it upon the Crown — when sufficiently steamed and dried they put it 10thly upon the block & brush & iron it upon a Table called the Hallboard, they use flat irons, the same as those for linnen which being many times rubbed over each part of the Hat with the assistance of a brush, smoothens and gives it a gloss; this is call'd dressing.-the edges are lastly cut even; & linings put into the Crown by Women; who also bind the Hats. The Linings are bought ready cut out which is a trade in Manchester and dying them another.

The final blocking of the hat, arrangement of the brim would be done by the hatter to which these felt shapes were sent, from whom they were distributed to the home and export markets.

Hatting in England had become such a large and prosperous trade that in 1784 the elder Pitt, looking desperately for further cash sources, was successful in putting a tax on hats, payable by the hatter, and confirmed by first a stamp, and then a ticket in the lining. It was not lifted until 1811. Despite constant evasion it was useful income for the government in their fight against the French, with whom they had been so acrimoniously sharing the overseas export markets.

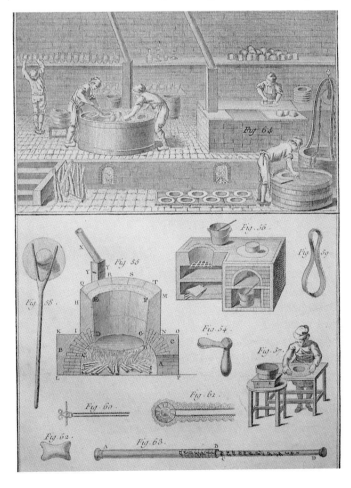

Left: The dyeing and final finishing of felt hats. The blocks and hats are ranged on the shelf above the workers. The loops, hooks and buttons, which help to hold the shape and provide a trim, are also shown. Notice the clogs worn by the men to protect them from the hot damp floor.

The early 19th century

For the fashionable man and woman about town at the beginning of the 19th century, there were a wealth of hat styles from which to choose. A desire for the classical principles of order and an increased personal awareness had been stimulated by the social and political turmoil of the recent past. In the international scene the Revolutionary wars and the Napoleonic wars were turning attention onto the cultures and ways of life of different countries.

Fifty years later, the battles lost and won, the Jury Report of the Great Exhibition of All Nations (1851) could note that "though the hat is an article of fashion . . . [it is] of such constant use it does not appear to be easy to change the habits and tastes of wearers or to induce them to adopt a new costume." It was referring to the top hat and the bonnet, which we see as the symbols of the Victorian world. The top hat is considered to convey authority and ambition, its shape to be a monument to the chimneys of the Industrial Revolution. The bonnet is seen as essential to the formation of the ideal Victorian woman, dependent, decorative, nonintellectual and submissive. It blinkered her view of the world, and its restrictive shape appeared to separate head from body. Like other summary judgments on Victorian society, this illustrates only part of a changing picture.

By the end of the 18th century, the trend towards simplicity and classicism was affecting the whole of a woman's appearance. Slim-fitting, high-waisted dresses in pale shades recalled the drapes and tunics of Ancient Greece and Rome. Hairstyles were arranged close to the head, and the hair with an artfully artless simplicity was either cut short or arranged in a soft knot at the crown. With a new "democratic" informality of manners hats and caps began to be worn more for effect than for etiquette and convention, though these were increasingly factors in the life of most women.

For outdoor wear, the most popular head covering was the hat or bonnet, which since classical models were in short supply was inspired by the rural style, the military and the romantic. The Gypsy bonnet was very popular, and blended the rural and the romantic trends. It was tubular, and had ribbons tied across the crown, bending it into what we now consider the bonnet shape. Helmet hats and bonnets had multinational inspirations from the classical with a brimlike peak to the conical line of the contemporary Hungarian shako. At the beginning of the century they were worn upright on the head, but when they began to be tilted

Above: Winter Fashions for 1840 from *Les Modes*. The lady's bonnet is so large that it conceals her profile and severely limits her view of the world. The man's top hat echoes the architectural features of the age, an aspect explored in J Laver, *Taste and Fashion*.

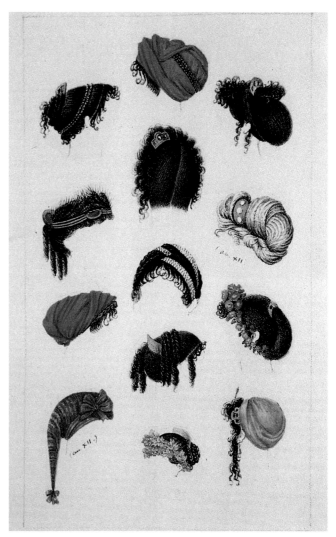

further back they projected in front to the extent that those wearing these vast "pokes" completely disappeared from view, and were caricatured in 1812 as Les Invisibles. As the curve around the face widened, the shape of the bonnet as we know it began to appear. For formal occasions the classical cap-cum-snood was much worn as well as exotic modes such as the Mameluke turban inspired by the Egyptian campaign. The neat feather-trimmed curves of the Elizabeth Valois hat reflected the craze for a romanticized past.

During the wars English and French fashions developed independently despite the "Fashionable Intelligence" from Paris which regularly crossed the battle lines. The United States' ties with France were close and there are many excellent French-style caps from this period in American museums.

At the Treaty of Paris (1815), when the international fashionable met, the differences in French and English style were noticed and satirized, and can be seen among the drawings by "Carle" Vernet engraved in *Le Bon Genre* (1815).

Initially the English were shocked at French fashions. To Lady Charlotte Bury, in 1814, "The ugliest part of the habillements is the high chimneys on their heads, which chimneys are covered with feathers and flowers." They were soon persuaded, and the style was quickly adopted in England. It balanced the new fashion line with a higher, tighter waist and a shorter skirt swung out at the ankle with frills. The trimmings were a feature, and a profusion of high piled, wired loops and bows decorate the bonnets of the 1820s and 1830s.

Above: Hats and headdresses from 1801; *Coiffures et rubans à l'Italienne et coiffures grecques,* **all in the fashionable classical style.**

Above left: London dresses for 1808. In the classical style, they are pale-colored and have a high waist. The lady on the right wears a straw hat, in the middle a flat, country-style straw shape with ribbon tie, on the left a turban.

Above: Hyde Park walking dress of 1812, from the Ladies Magazine. It is in the fashionable military style, and the hat is a close copy of an officer's bicorne. Even the muff manages to resemble a bearskin cap.

Above right: "Les Modernes Incroyables," from *Caricatures Parisiennes,* 1810, illustrate the ridiculous extreme of masculine fashion. Hats are of all shapes, bicornes, and very high and very low top hats.

Right: The contrast between English and French fashions was satirized in 1815 by Carle Vernet for the series *Costumes Anglais et Français,* for *Le Bon Genre.* Tall frilly bonnets were a feature of French fashion and soon to be copied by the English.

By the mid-1820s bonnets became wider as the dresses developed a new horizontal emphasis: the sleeves broadened, the waist dropped and the skirt widened. The look was summarized by the satirists as "Waist and Extravagance."

It was the custom to wear hats and high trimmed caps for all occasions and a French theater manager coped with blocked views of the stage by asking all attractive ladies to remove their hats; others could retain them.

The extravagance was not maintained. In the mid-1830s as the shoulder line tightened and the waist was lowered in a V, so the bonnet adopted a more open rounded brim which framed the face, and the crown shortened.

In England and the United States the Cottage bonnet was the most popular, its crown merging imperceptibly with the brim which extended beyond the profile, curving down at the side to cover the ears and frame the cheeks. The Bibi was fashionable in France, wide and light as the name suggests, a frivolous childish nonsense.

In the home, caps were worn. They were high to cover the hair which since before the 1820s had been built up on the crown of the head. Made from fine lawn, check muslin and tulle and trimmed with lace, insertions and gauged flounces, they have a lighthearted charm and were usually washable though laundering them required skill in the use of puffing and goffering irons, no longer in the domestic repertoire. Even in their own time, they were treated with care, and there are many in costume collections.

Top: A millinery shop in Paris drawn by Chalon in 1822. The young girls are trimming the hats in an open booth.

Above: A French straw top hat, about 1820. They were popular continental middle-class summer wear.

Above: The fashions of 1828 drawn for Benjamin Read. The fashionable ladies viewing the Colosseum in Regents Park wear wide-brimmed, extravagantly trimmed hats, the men top hats in fawn and black. Their shapes are far more varied than they were to be later in the century.

Right: *Waist and Extravagance,* a satirical look at the extremes of the mode by W. Heath, about 1830. Highly trimmed hats were a feature.

Above left: Hats and bonnets of about 1830, engraved for *"Psyche," Journal des Modes,* by "Numa." The bonnets have deep brims and high angled crowns. On the left in the middle row is an evening headdress made from tucked ribbon and below is an indoor cap. On the top right and at the middle bottom are children's hats.

Left: Elaborate indoor caps were popular with most married women in the 1830s. Agnes Frazier, painted by an unknown artist in about 1835, wears a fine and fashionable example.

Above: A fashion plate of 1830. The hat recommended for informal day wear is very elaborately trimmed and its width balances the broad shoulder line.

During the 18th century it had been the custom to wear caps under hats but this was no longer possible; there was not the space. Hats and caps were worn alternately and in small towns such as Mrs. Gaskell's fictional Cranford it was quite usual to see ladies going to evening parties wearing their hats, and with their bonnets, "new got up" for the occasion in bonnet baskets and boxes. Such large and elaborate confections in any case required careful storage, and this is the period when the large, attractive bonnet or bandbox came into its own, and many examples still survive.

Hats and bonnets were bought from milliners or *Marchands des Modes* either ready or part-trimmed. The Paris milliner reigned supreme and the *Almanach des Modes* of 1821 listed them for foreign visitors; Mlle. Fanny of the Rue des Ménars was considered the smartest; Mme. Herbault was sometimes too bold, but popular with foreign courts; the best was Mme. Guèrin, known for the richness of her silks, the effect of her ribbons, the subtlety of her flowers and the arrangement of her turbans. She worked with Mme. Victorine whose confections, by mid-century, were to adorn the head of Queen Victoria.

Not all women either wanted or could afford to buy their bonnets. Styling was easier as ladies' magazines included more illustrations; hats could be sketched surreptitiously at parties and copied from window displays. Most ladies, and certainly their maids, could sew, and the flowers and trimmings could cover a multitude of errors. Jane Austen was very bonnet-conscious and often refers to styles in her correspondence as well as in her novels. In 1797, she writes to her sister that she has changed the black feather on her silver-ribbon-trimmed evening cap for "coquelicot [poppy] . . . all the fashion this winter" but feeling as "I should not prosper if I strayed from your directions," she changed it back.

Many instruction books were printed for those less skilled than Jane Austen. Mme. Celnart was a popular instructress of the 1820s and 1830s. In her *Manuel des Dames* (1829), she gives advice on the making of toques, hats without brims generally mounted on a band; turbans, bandeaux around which were wrapped squares of material; and bonnets, always made of gauze or net and suitable for women of a "certain age" and limited means; soft caps for the elegant young; and finally the Scotch cap, which she found completely ridiculous. In England, these Tam-O'-Shanter bonnets were very popular and merged with the romantic modes drawn from the inspiration of Sir Walter Scott's novels. They were still fashionable when Mrs. Howell added her advice in the *Handbook of Millinery* (1847). She adds instructions on the construction of the Cottage or Drawn Bonnet, the inspiration of the sunbonnet which was to remain in the country-woman's wardrobe on both sides of the Atlantic until well into the 20th century. It resembled the Calache of the previous century in being made from fabric stiffened by strips of cane or whalebone.

Most home milliners used papier mâché millinery heads for making bonnets. They were busts with the head extended with a conical leather cap and prissy painted features, of which many still survive. However, only a few of the many bonnets remain and almost none in an unaltered condition. They have lost their linings and their facings, the correct color of which was supposed to complement those long-gone complexions. The delicate ruches of tulle or lace around the inside of the brim, the last vestiges of the cap frill, have crumbled to dust, and the ribbons and flowers have been rearranged or replaced for fancy dress or amateur dramatics.

What we have is the shape, usually made from straw, braided, stitched and blocked into shape. The ordinary chip, white paille de riz (willow chip), crinoline and spartary are less often found.

The early 19th century was the boom period of the straw hat industry in

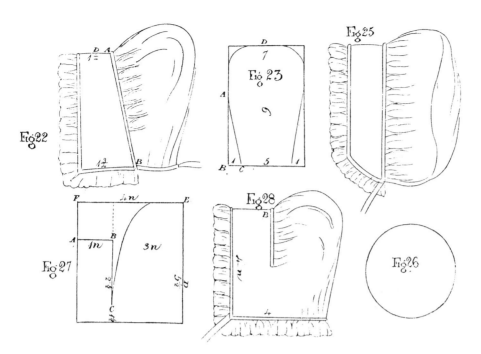

Left: Patterns for caps from *The Workwoman's Guide*, 1836/40. Despite their simplicity, and they were intended for informal wear, servants and the poor, they have the fashionable line, full on the crown to accommodate the hair knotted on the top of the head.

Below: Hats of 1863, a very early fashion photograph from the catalogue of a London shop, Peter Robinson. Although they are for mourning wear, the shapes are chic, small "fanchon" bonnets, just covering the top of the head.

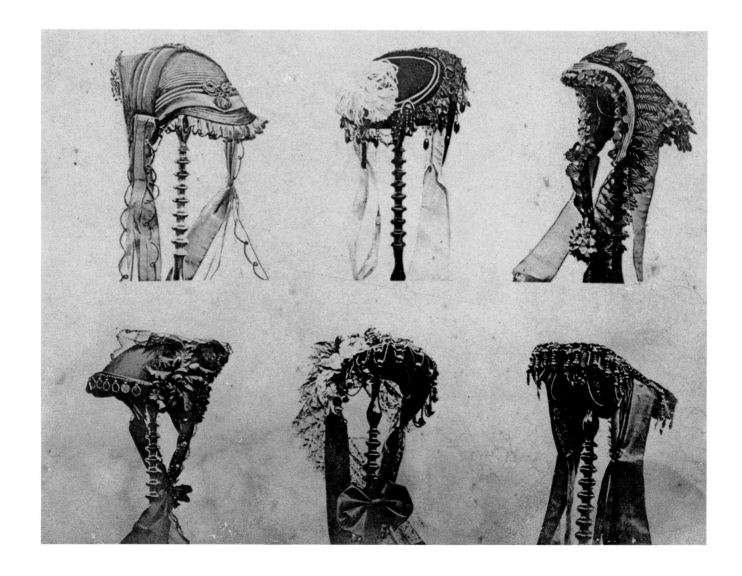

England and also in the United States. By the end of the 18th century, it reached high-fashion status, when the wars began to affect the supply from Italy where Leghorn and Florence made the highest quality fashion hats. As luxuries, Italian straw hats were highly taxed. Making homegrown alternatives meant finding a substitute for the unique *Tritium turgidum*, the bearded wheat native to Piedmont and seemingly impossible to grow elsewhere. The Royal Society of Arts prizes inspired many substitutes and the interruption in supply stimulated much initiative. In America one of Betsey Metcalfe's bonnets had adorned the head of the wife of President John Quincy Adams, and what has been called "the Tiffany of 19th-century United States straw bonnet making" was Stoddard and Knowlton of West Upton, Massachusetts.

The problem of finding a suitable fiber was partially solved in England when the Machine or Sheen was introduced, around 1800, much quicker than Betsey Metcalfe's scissors at shredding the straw into chips. Faceted heads fixed at right angles to the handle could be pushed through the hollow straw, splitting it into equal strands; they were ingenious, cheap and effective. By the 1830s, in the Austin machine, they had been grouped, several cutting heads to a frame.

The economists marveled at the difference between the cost of the material and price of finished product: $1 of outlay could bring in $20 profit. Generally the making of the plait was piecework, something an out-worker could do in odd moments, though soon it became a full-time occupation even involving the so-called "Plait Schools," often a Dickensian-like mixture of substandard day nursery, minimal education and sweated child labor. Though the process was basic, skill was essential. Moistening the straw strands as necessary, usually with her lips, the plaiter braided the strips. The patterns were varied and a good worker could make 15 to 20 yards a day. However as demand increased and duties were lowered it became more economical to import ready-made straw braid from Italy and the native strawplaiting trade began to die. The bonnets were made up in small cottage workshops and brought to warehouses where they were blocked and sometimes partially trimmed, from which they were dispatched. Increasingly, Luton in Bedfordshire, convenient for London and the railroad, was becoming an important millinery base.

Right: The domestic craft of making straw hats from braid changed little over the years. This painting by C. A. Smith, 1891, illustrates outworkers in their cottage, near Luton, Bedfordshire. The old lady makes the plait, the younger women sew the hats.

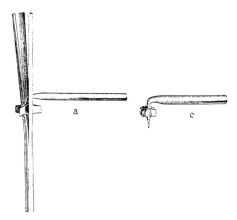

During the postwar period when countries were fighting for a share in the straw hat market, there was a great interchange of techniques. With Royal Society of Arts encouragement, in 1822 John Parry introduced a bonded plait on the Italian model, avoiding the wasteful ridges left by the English method of overlapping the braid. In 1834, T.B. Smith of St. Albans introduced a Brazilian plait which, like the Panama hat, was woven in one piece from the crown. The Italians borrowed English fashions and instead of the flat shapes they had been making, introduced bonnet shapes which were very popular, especially in France. There was also competition from Switzerland where a new industry was beginning to make delicate combinations of braid-woven straw and horsehair. The shape of the bonnet improved as gelatin was introduced for stiffening. After the straw began to be bleached with peroxide instead of sulfur, brighter, more varied dyes were used.

In the early 1850s, the Cottage bonnet had begun to relax its inhibiting limitation of a woman's view of the world. Becoming shorter from crown to brim, it began to be worn further back on the head, and widened, framing the

Above left: Straw braid from Luton, Bedfordshire. There were many different forms of plaits.

Above: Straw splitters, introduced in the early 19th century, were the hand tools needed to split the tubular corn stalks into equal strips suitable for plaiting. The star-shaped blades were metal or bone. This type was used in Luton, Bedfordshire.

Left: A bonnet of the late 1840s, made from a combination of crinoline, a horsehair braid and fancy straw, and trimmed with silk lace, artificial flowers and ribbon. It is one of the few surviving bonnets to retain the trimming on the underside of the brim. It is labeled "Mrs Bell, milliner, 34 Wigmore Street, Hanover Square," a good address and a smart, long-established shop.

Above: *Derby Day 1858*, by W. P. Frith, illustrates a cross-section of English society in their best clothes for a day at the races. In the middle is a fashionable group, the ladies with small "fanchon" bonnets and wide straw hats. The men wear top hats and one, lounging by the carriage, has a veil to protect him from the sun. On the right, in the non-fashionable group, is a country man with a soft, round felt hat.

Right: Day and informal dress engraved for *Le Magasin des Familles*, 1851, by Heloise Leloir. The bonnets, less deep than in the 1840s, have a slightly flaring brim and *bavolets* to shade the nape of the neck. The small girl is dressed like a bride for her First Communion.

face instead of enclosing it. In general straw bonnets were now confined to spring and summer, and shapes covered with silk or velvet were worn in the winter. For semi-formal occasions, lace and frills echo the trimming of the wide crinoline-supported skirt.

Hairstyles were becoming a feature in the later 1850s, dressed up in the front, puffing out at the side, and low at the back. To accommodate this new style, bonnets became smaller and triangular with no demarcation between brim and crown. These *Fanchon* bonnets, so called from the French for banner, were made without *Bavolets*, the frill which had formerly concealed the back of the neck, an innovation credited to Charles Worth, the Paris couturier.

However, there were valid alternatives to the bonnet. In 1851, as part of her attempt to reform dress, Amelia Bloomer had included a wide-brimmed straw hat with the tunic and trouser outfit that she suggested. Bloomers as such were laughed out of existence but the hat remained, though mainly worn by children and for country wear. As conventions began to relax in the mid-1850s, so this informal hat began to be accepted for town wear, though considered essentially youthful and emancipated. The fashion for hats, as opposed to bonnets, increased, and by the 1860s on their neatly coiffed heads, the Young Girl of the Period, or Fast Young Lady as she had begun to be called by those worried about her brash and emancipated attitudes, was wearing hats and leaving bonnets to the more mature.

The focus of the hairstyle was now an enormous knot of hair emphasizing the back of the head, and the hats were small and tipped forward over the brow. The styling was masculine: pillbox caps borrowed from that popular hero of Italian nationalism, Giuseppe Garibaldi; pork-pies, the masculine Bollinger, a miniature bowler in style. The charm was in contrast. Shrewd M. Le Blanc in the *Art in Ornament* (1877) was to note "something rather masculine or military in the

Above: *Croquet Players,* **painted by Winslow Homer, 1866; the girls wear up-to-date, forward-tilted hats, the man a straw sailor hat.**

headdress . . . [provides] . . . an air of bravado which contrasts with the delicacy of her sex." A fashionable idol of the age was the Irish-Parisian courtesan Skittles. Debonair, a good horsewoman, her brash charm did much to establish the popularity of the pork-pie hat.

Queen Victoria had never really been a style-setter, though in youth she was as interested in fashion as any other young person. But after Prince Albert's death in 1861, as a widow, she spent 40 years in mourning, and set a vogue for royal anti-fashion, institutional dressing which lingered well into the 20th century.

The rules for mourning had been set by the early 15th century and confirmed in the following centuries. Colorless garments, black and white, with a dull finish, were the norm and especially for the widow, the custom was complete segregation, modified in modern society to concealment under caps, hats and veils. Queen Victoria's cap, pointed over the brow, was based on a portrait of Mary Queen of Scots. Her daughter, the widowed Empress of Prussia, wore one in black. Confirmed and restated by commercial interests, the widows of England were advised that respectable mourning should last for at least two and a half years, thereafter modulating very slightly to half mourning. In the later 19th century, the rules were restated and confirmed by commercial pressures. Family mourning extended to the ultimate limits of kinship, and among the ruling classes there was also sympathetic mourning, especially for royal personages. The subject is documented in Lou Taylor's *Mourning Dress: a Costume and Social History* (1983). The white widow's cap, tight around the face with pendant lappets, sometimes also called weepers, and the black widow's bonnet, surmounting the acres of sepulchral crepe, became symbols of an age in which women took responsibility for making social statements on behalf of the family.

Below: Men's French fashions for 1865; a sporty tweed suit with a high-crowned hard felt hat; a formal tail coat with a tall shiny top hat; semiformal frock coat with a grey top hat.

Below right: Queen Victoria wears the pointed widow's cap with dangling veil-like weepers for her portrait by J. von Angeli in 1875. She wore mourning clothes and this type of cap from the death of Prince Albert in 1861 to her own in 1901.

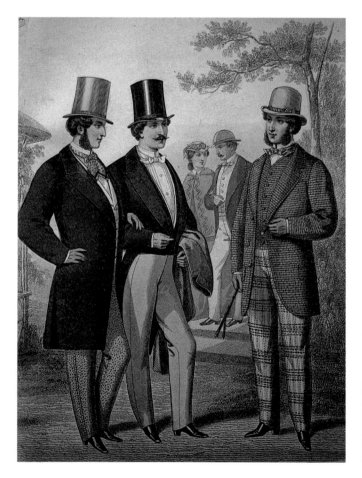

Middle–of–the–road fashion was set by the young members of the Royal family. Alexandra, Princess of Wales, had been a charming model for the changing styles since she stepped on English soil in 1861, and continued to lead fashion through the 1870s. The early photographs of her in day clothes, available copiously and inexpensively in *Carte de Visite*, did much to publicize suave off–the–face Fanchon bonnets, followed in the later 1860s and 1870s by neat, forward–tilted pork–pie hats. Always elegant, her day clothes are usually plain. Hats and all types of accessories were named after her, but their inspiration was general, rather than any particular endorsement of her personal style. She enjoyed outdoor pursuits, and no doubt many Englishwomen hoped that they looked equally charming in masculine tweed shooting caps and jaunty straw sailor hats. Alexandra herself had many rivals for leadership in the European fashion stakes. With the development of smart sporty outdoor hats, it is interesting that the ineffably chic Empress Eugènie of France and the beautiful Elizabeth, Empress of Austria, both dressed by Worth, were even fonder of outdoor pursuits than she. Eugènie's long country walks were the bane of the life of her Ladies in Waiting, and the Empress Elizabeth, in strict hunting gear, rigidly whaleboned, polished top hat, and, as she became older, ever thicker hunting veil, had a sinister, deviant appeal that went beyond fashion.

Alexandra's image became sterotyped as she aged, but as her fashion influence on the younger set waned, her husband's increased. By the end of the century it was Edward, Prince of Wales, who was the style leader, not the Princess, especially the Prince enjoying himself in holiday clothes.

The rest of the English royal family never had the same fashionable charisma; the smart ladies of England were seeking more escapist dreams than The Home Life of Our Dear Queen Victoria.

The mood of the 1870s was romantic, a return to the ancien régime of Louis XVI. The hats and bonnets of the 1870s clung precariously to an ever–rising hairstyle. Lamballe hats, called after the Duchesse de Lamballe, friend of Marie Antoinette, and Dolly Varden bonnets, named after Dolly Varden, the heroine of Dickens's *Barnaby Rudge*, set in the 1770s, complemented the looped–up panier–style dresses and high buckled shoes which were simulating the styles of a hundred years before.

At the end of the 18th century, there were only two style choices for men. The Cap of Liberty was no more and for those who wished to build a new society there was a choice between the cocked hat of the ancien régime and the stiff tapering hat. Most men used both, wearing the flat cocked hat for formal occasions and the other for everyday. In France, the bicorne cocked hat became particularly associated with the young reactionary middle class, the Incroyables of the Directoire. In its military version it has become well known to us as worn by Napoleon.

By the beginning of the 19th century, the top hat began its long career. The height of the felt hat had grown and the silhouette was changing. Some hats were conical, others concave and others retained the tapering form. Nor was the brim always the same: it could be wide, narrow or gently curled. All these elements were mingled as the taste of the wearer or his hatter decided, and the shapes which resulted were given the names of those who had sponsored or inspired them; thus the Wellington hat differed from the Cumberland hat and both from that of Beau Brummel. They could be white, beige or brown as well as black. Only the best and most expensive hats were now made completely of beaver. Some were "plated," that is, given a beaver top layer, others were made from hare or rabbit, sometimes with an admixture of wool. The main difference between them and those later in the century was the finish.

Above: Hunting dress of 1830, engraved for *La Mode* by Gavarni. The hunting outfit has changed little within the past 150 years, though reinforcement of the cap is now considered an essential feature.

Right: Top hats, 1830–1900. At left the high fur felt "stovepipe" with polished surface; middle, a beige felt of about 1830 with the crown shape known as the "Wellington"; right, a silk plush hat with mourning band of about 1890.

There is a frequently repeated story that in January 1797 a City of London hatter, John Heathcote, caused a riot by appearing in a "Tall structure having a shiny lustre and calculated to frighten people." If not entirely apocryphal, the story points up the main difference between the early top hat and those of the later period: their finish. The good hats of the early part of the century had the kind of gloss which could be achieved with expertly polished fur felt. The really glossy hat did not appear until silk pile fabric began to be used for its surface. Now, in the late 20th century, melusine, the silk pile fabric, is no longer produced, and top hats are made from fine hare fur felt.

John Melton, Hatter to the Heads of the People, wrote a retrospective account of the trade in 1853. Looking back to the early days of the century he remembered the upper classes as being reluctant to accept the early hats which had a silk fabric fixed on a felt base. Making these is said to have been an Italian technique introduced in the 1770s. The hats were very clumsy, heavy and did not take an elegant shape. The alternative of using a whalebone– or cane–supported crown was also tried, but unsuccessfully. It was not until the 1830s, when stiffened muslin foundations began to be used, a French innovation, that these problems were overcome. The best melusine covers came from France and were popular at the top end of the trade, despite high duties, and in England, for more ordinary qualities there were silks woven in Spitalfields, Coventry and Banbury.

Once the problem of manufacture had been solved, the sales of the silk hat soon outstripped those of the stuff hat. It was partly fashion, but it was also price. Made with new techniques, by different workers and using new materials they were a quarter the cost of the traditional felt. Flimsiness, poor dye and lack of durability did not matter; style had become universally available. A man's hat no longer had to be a consumer durable. And, for those who could not afford the price of a new hat, which soon became far less expensive, there were secondhand ones.

There had always been a sale for secondhand felts, even though the trade had tried to regulate it, but reblocking a Gossamer, as silk hats were also called, was very much easier to do. The secondhand clothes dealer with a pile of hats on his head was soon a familiar sight and Henry Mayhew, in his *London Life and the London Poor* (1851/1862), has much to say on how they were collected, handled and then sold. They were very popular on Saturday nights, ready for church on Sunday. Photography, the new visual record of the period shows them on the head of everyman.

Taking up more space, they were more inconvenient than the flatter hats of the 18th century, particularly at a time when there were no cloakrooms in theaters or other places of entertainment. At the end of the evening, there was often a terrible scramble for hats. Many attempted to solve the problem, by inventing a

Left: French sporting dress of the 1840s. The wide-brimmed felt hat is a fashion for the young and romantic. The young man at the rear wears a flat cap based on military styles, which was to change little over the years.

collapsible hat which could be put in the pocket. Hats with folding foundations had been introduced as early as 1820, but it was not until Antoine Gibus, a Paris hatter, applied his ingenuity to the problem that it was solved. His patents, filed between 1834 and 1840, worked well, and indeed the name Gibus is one of those given to the folding opera hat.

For those who wanted something more dashing than the top hat there were wide–brimmed felts which could be worn with tweed suits in the country. To *Punch* in 1840, they were "wide awakes because they had no nap," but their links were with general country styling. They were very similar to the romantic wide–brimmed hats which were being worn by students in the revolutionary Europe of the 1840s, and which were indeed specifically forbidden in Germany at the height of democratic unrest. A variety known as the Kossuth, after Lajos Kossuth, leader of the Hungarian independence movement, was briefly the fashion in America and England which he visited in 1851.

In the United States their dashing charm was confirmed by the revival of the style in the 1860s, when a broad–brimmed felt was worn by soldiers on both sides during the American Civil War. Variants passed into general use as the Cowboy hat and when worn by Theodore Roosevelt's roughriders in the Spanish–American War of 1890, that name was given to it. In England it was the wear of the irregular soldiers in the South African war, and of Canadian, New Zealand and Australian soldiers in the present century. As cowboy hat, it blends usefulness with romantic charisma, and it is also the early version Boy Scout hat.

In the United States the broad–brimmed styles were supplemented by many varieties of straw, into which it was the aim of the hatter to get city men to change at the beginning of every summer. In England, however, straw hats were aristocratic rather than democratic until the end of the century when the Boater was introduced.

For informal wear in town there was the Bowler which the long–established and aristocratic firm of hatters, Locke's of St. James, had introduced in the 1850s.

Initially it was a variation of the Thanet, a type of medium–high felt, riding and country hat which William Coke, later Earl of Leicester, a Norfolk landowner used to order for himself and his gamekeepers for wearing on the estate. The innovation lay in the reduction of the height, which made it less likely to catch in the branches. In Locke's records it is described as "a hard fur felt with a semi rough finish."

It was not the form which gave it the name of Bowler, but the firm of feltmakers commissioned by Locke's to make the original hood, Thomas and William Bowler of Southwark. It soon became popular with men who wanted something easier than the top hat and less informal than the wideawake. It did much to re-establish the felt industry which had gone into decline.

The firm disclaims the association of the hat with the name Billycock, however apt this may seem, and a lengthy correspondence in the London *Telegraph* in 1950, established two origins for the term; a wide–brimmed hat following the style of cocked brim adopted by gangs of upperclass hooligans in late 18th–century London; a protective hat worn by tin miners in Cornwall and made by a local hatter, William Coke. Nevertheless despite learned controversy, the term Billycock is indissolubly linked with the Bowler and no doubt this association will, through usage, be one day as valid as any other.

Another variation of the style with a flat brim, was commissioned by the Duke of Cambridge in 1865 and was called the Cambridge after him, becoming well–known to the public when it was worn by Winston Churchill at the beginning of his political career. A distinctive gray version was chosen by the Earl of Derby at the race at which it was conventional to wear formally informal dress. It was his popularization of it which spread news of this useful alternative to the Top Hat to the United States. By the end of the century in the United States a Derby will be much more widely worn than the Top Hat. In England, the more democratic version of the round felt was the Bollinger, a shallow domed felt with a button on the crown, which is often seen in photographs of dashing army men in mufti, and was said to have been popular with bus and cab drivers.

But there was still a need for a useful soft cap, such as had been met in the 16th century by the flat cap and in the 17th and 18th centuries by the Montero. After the Napoleonic wars it was filled by army surplus. The author of the *Art of Dress* (1830), observed "with disgust boys and the lower orders generally, wearing army and navy regulation caps . . with the utmost nonchalance as though perfectly ignorant of . . . the honour they were sullying . . . low apprentice lads with . . . naval caps with cheek pieces down shuffling about diverse holiday places".

The upper classes, unwilling to don wartime cast-offs, wore soft paneled caps with tassles and peaks rather like those of continental students, for informal sporting use. Moving down the social scale, they became plainer, and merged with the more comfortable and less flamboyant military styles of mid century such as the Engineer's peaked cap and the French army soft forage cap.

MERCURY AND THE MAD HATTER

The phrase "Mad as a Hatter" has been common in the English language ever since Lewis Carroll wrote of the Mad Hatter's Tea Party in his famous children's tale *Alice in Wonderland*, published in 1865. Dictionaries refer to the possibility that "hatter" in the phrase is a corruption of an early English phrase "mad as an adder," using the old meaning of angry, still in use in the United States. A little deeper investigation, however, makes it clear that Carroll was referring to the recently identified industrial disease caused by inhaling the fumes of mercuric nitrate, a mixture used certainly since the mid-18th century, for felting of animal furs for hat-making.

John Simon, Medical Officer to the British Privy Council, had set out a whole range of industrial diseases affecting the English working classes, and through intensive propaganda and parliamentary activity had succeeded in getting the Factory Act of 1864 passed, which among other things, required proper ventilation in workshops. *Alice in Wonderland* was published a year after the act was passed, and certainly Carroll, an Oxford don, was likely to have known about Simon's work in general.

Hatters had suffered from this complaint ever since "secret" processes for felting had been introduced in the early 18th century – first becoming irritable, getting upset at the slightest thing, being embarrassed when asked about their work, and generally behaving not like the Hatter at the Tea Party, but just like the Hatter when being tried by the King in a later scene; the King notices that the Hatter looks uneasy and anxious, and trembles so that he took both his shoes off – "Don't be nervous," says the king, "or I'll have you executed on the spot!" The symptoms described by Carroll are precisely those identified in the early stages of the disease.

In *L'Art de faire des chapeaux* published in France in 1765, the author F. Nollet refers to the secret felting process which had been used since 1752, and which he described as having been introduced from England. Typically there are English references to the process having been brought to England from France by Huguenots after their expulsion in 1687 by the Edict of Nantes! There is no doubt that the mercury treatment was in use on both sides of the English Channel, and that workers in felting were known to become a bit peculiar.

In the United States the same symptoms were observed among hatters during the mid-19th century, and were soon known as the Danbury Shakes, from the name of the Connecticut town of Danbury, in Fairfield County, which was famous for its hat and silk manufacturers.

The illness develops through the inhalation by the workers of the felt dust which is being treated with mercuric nitrate. The fine hairs used in fur felt came from rabbits, hares, muskrats and beavers, and are smooth, resilient and straight. It was found that when dipped into an acid solution of mercuric nitrate they became limp, twisted and rough, thus making the felting process much easier and more effective. Working in ill-ventilated workshops the fumes and the dust were inhaled by the workers, gradually, often over a number of years, affecting their movements, leading eventually to a definite tremble or shake, to such an extent that it became difficult even for them; to walk before there was any protection for workers or any proper medical diagnosis, they went on working, even if they had to be led to their workbench because they were incapable of getting to it without assistance.

The only item in Carroll's tale that might be slightly wrong is the price tag on the Mad Hatter's top hat – 10/6d (ten shillings and sixpence, or half a guinea in the old British coinage). A very expensive hat for an English hatter in the 1860s – a "four and niner" at half that price – would have been more appropriate, but then, though full of hidden truths, Alice after all, was a fairy tale.

The later nineteenth century

In the later 19th century, fashionable hats reached all levels of society. Expectations altered as leisure slowly increased and holidays became part of the general pattern of life. Transport and communications improved, shopping habits changed and a slow but general rise in wages gave people more money to spend. Women, sensitive barometers of social change, began to modify their self-image. With better education, they became more self-confident and were well on their way to becoming the New Woman. Shops and new office jobs provided alternatives to the drudgery that had been the lot of women for so long. More than ever before, the single working woman had money in her pocket. In

Right: *At the Milliners* by Edgar Degas, about 1883. Buying a new hat had become a feminine ritual by the later 19th century and Paris the heart of the fashionable socialite's world.

response to this, the working man had to sharpen his image in order to appeal. The new inexpensive illustrated magazines were not slow to link consumer and advertiser, and opened up a new world of entertainment on the way. As the young began to claim the right to a dream world, the media were quick to suggest that a shortcut to wish fulfilment was a new hat and by the beginning of the 20th century, the bioscope, the forerunner of the cinema, was providing images of a wider world and a whole new galaxy of fashion immortals.

By the mid-1870s, women's dress was still inspired by historical models, and through the decade moved from the rounded curves of Louis Seize to the straight lines of the directoire. The hair was styled to enhance the new, more elongated, slimmer silhouette. Instead of being massed over the forehead it began to be piled at the back of the head. Hats, which had been perched precariously over the forehead, were poised towards the back, with shape and trimmings emphasizing the effect of height. In sympathy with the fashionable mood, the shapes of hats became defined. Wired shapes covered with frills were replaced with felts and dense woven straws. The toque and the postillion, based on the late 18th-century gentleman's round hat, with conical crown and narrow brim, were popular, and the Gainsborough for those with more romantic tastes, with asymmetric curled brim trimmed with feathers. Bonnets were worn for more formal occasions and by older women. The shapes and the strings were decorative, merely perched on the back of the head, but as the ever-perceptive M. Le Blanc pointed out, they gave the "appearance of modesty because they showed at least the intention of covering the part which is exposed."

By the mid-1880s the feminine silhouette was angular and almost square. The

Above left: An indoor dress and cap and a half-mourning visiting outfit worn with a hat, as illustrated in a fashion plate of 1871.

Above: Alexandra, Princess of Wales, was photographed with her son in the late 1870s wearing a feminine version of a man's shooting cap with her neat tweed sports suit.

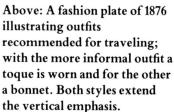

Above: A fashion plate of 1876 illustrating outfits recommended for traveling; with the more informal outfit a toque is worn and for the other a bonnet. Both styles extend the vertical emphasis.

Above right: *A Ball on Shipboard* **by J. Tissot, 1874, illustrates fashionable informal dress. The identically dressed girls, perhaps sisters, wear sailor hats with their matching outfits, and the elegant lady in the foreground wears a flower-trimmed, bonnet-like hat. The men sport informal felts and straws.**

waistline had risen and the bustle replaced the sleek draped hipline. To compensate, the hats rose even higher, perched foursquare on the neat tight hairstyles. An extreme example was known as "Four Stories and a Basement." The trimmings were architectural in their clarity of form but naturalistic, horticultural, zoological and even entomological in content. In 1878, "wormeaten faded green leaves are among the most natural things in spring millinery" and "Trimmings of hats and bonnets include not only those insects and birds which appeal to our sense of beauty but those which cause a revulsion of feeling such as spiders, water beetles, caterpillars and even lizards and toads," and the fashion plates confirm this; lobsters look down from bonnets, beetles crawl up.

It seems to have been a case of loving the animal world to death. Dr. C. Willett Cunnington, costume authority and Freudian, associated the craze for zoological decoration with the sublimation of sexual desire among women doomed to late marriage in a time of economic slump. Redirected affections are also credited with the philanthropic and conservationist movements which were also a feature of the age. The conservationist American Audubon Society was founded in 1886 and the English Royal Society for the Preservation of Birds in 1889. The consumption of feathers for hat decoration was enormous, and the literature of the preservation societies recites with conscious bloodcurdling effect, stories of birds massacred by the millions. Herons and egrets so much prized for graceful tail feathers, were particularly vulnerable, especially when rearing young. Bloodstained feathered mothers and starving baby chicks brought frissons of horror into the Victorian boudoir. There was also the grebe, almost exterminated in the search for its dense silky breast plumage, chic trimmings for muff and collar as well as hat.

The campaign attracted influential patronage and in 1906 Alexandra, when Queen, agreed to forbid the use of osprey plumage at court. Ostrich feathers, which had always been very popular, were not considered a problem by the conservationists. It was said that they could be removed without hurting the bird and ostrich farms, an English initiative, were first founded in Cape Colony, South Africa, in 1865, and by the 1880s were in full production. It is sad that so many birds were destroyed for the color and texture of their plumage, just at a time when dyestuff technology made it feasible to recolor feathers easily and effectively. Moreover, even feathers from the family hens were very adaptable in

Left: The tall, tapering hat was a feature of mid-1880s millinery, as this fashion plate from *Myra's Journal* of 1886 illustrates.

Below left: *Berthe,* in a pastel by J. Tissot, 1888, wears a fashionably tall hat with an exceptionally wide brim and elaborate trimming.

Below: Indoor caps from family photographs of the 1880s, when they were conventional wear for most respectable married women.

Illustrations of British Costume.

Above: A feather-trimmed toque of 1876, designed by Madame Dufourmantelle for *Le Caprice*, 1876. Realistic feather trimmings were the height of fashion.

Above middle: A fashionable, formally dressed couple in walking dress from *British Costume*, 1886. The hats on men and women were almost equally tall at this period. The lady's hat appears to have been trimmed with diving canaries.

Above right: Untrimmed hats and fur and feather mounts, as illustrated in *Le Caprice* in 1880. The owl mounts and stuffed ermine illustrate the macabre preferences of the period.

skilled hands.

The tail feathers of a cock and breast of a "white Brahmahen" were among the resources which were suggested to the girl being advised on *How to dress for £15 per year* in 1878, one of the many guides to life on limited means. She was allotted 3 bonnets and 2 hats, but at about 15/– [shillings] they were expensive. It was better to buy a shape at half this price and learn to do it yourself. It seems that old bonnets could be turned and cleaned at only 3/– [shillings]. All the shop catalogs include shapes and trimmings as well as ready-trimmed hats, and continued to do so until the 1920s.

From the middle of the 19th century, shop catalogs are a very useful way of charting fashion changes. The department store had begun to develop in the 1860s; in France the Bon Marché and Galeries Lafayette, in England Whiteleys was the earliest, followed by Peter Robinson, Liberty and Harrods, and in New York, there was Bloomingdale's and Stern's. Shopping on account and by post

Right: A fashionable crowd at Brighton in 1893, dressed formally for a seaside promenade—perhaps it was Sunday! Many of the men wear top hats, the women fashionable hats and bonnets.

was an important feature.

But the most systematic guidance is that from Montgomery Ward and Sears, Roebuck, the Chicago mail-order pioneers. Dream hats were always a feature of the Wish Books, and comparison between copies of the catalogs suggests that Sears' claim to provide the cheapest goods, and it is to be hoped, best value, can be justified. Their 1897 bonnets are half the price of the Bloomingdale's styles ten years previously. The most elaborate retailed at $2–$3 and the "shapes" at under a dollar.

Millinery fashion changed between the mid-1880s and mid-1890s in sympathy with a noticeable alteration in the line of the dress. The emphasis had shifted from hip to shoulder line, where the hitherto narrow sleeves were being given ballooning fullness at the top. The fashionable inspirations were now the rich hierarchic angular elegance of the Tudors and the delicate Biedermeier hourglass line of the 1830s.

Left: Five gentlemen's outfits shown in a Bloomingdale's advertisement, 1887. The hats are tall and tapering and confirm the fashionable line. The outfits include the Derby for the informal and semi-formal; tweed sack and cutaway suits; a soft tweed hat with a Norfolk sports outfit; a top hat with a formal frock coat.

Right: In 1897 Sears, Roebuck offered their first range of ladies' hats to the American public. They were economical and smart, with their tall crowns and straight brims balancing the rather rigid fashionable line of the period.

MILLINERY DEPARTMENT

WE TAKE PLEASURE IN DIRECTING THE ATTENTION OF OUR CUSTOMERS TO THIS VERY COMPLETE DEPARTMENT, including as it does a line of trimmed and untrimmed hats patterned after the latest novelties imported from Europe. Our buyers have been unusually fortunate in securing for the coming season a selection of millinery that has no equal in any ordinary retail store in the country. By importing in very large quantities, securing our goods from the leading manufacturers at home and abroad and selling on our one small profit plan direct to the consumer, we are able to in most cases sell to you a better class of goods than you can find in local retail stores, at about half the ordinary retail price. The illustrations in no instance do the goods justice, and we can only urge our customers to take advantage of our liberal terms and inspect any of the goods which they desire. We have every reason to believe that they will be delighted with the purchase and will be so well pleased with the goods that they will take pleasure in telling their friends where they have secured them and the unusually low price paid.

OUR LIBERAL TERMS. ON RECEIPT OF $1.00 WITH ORDER we will send any trimmed or untrimmed hat C. O. D. subject to examination. You can examine it at the express office, and if found exactly as represented, pay the express agent the balance with express charges and the goods are yours; otherwise return them at our expense and we will cheerfully refund your money. Three per cent discount allowed if cash in full accompanies your order. This discount will in many cases be sufficient to partially pay the express. It is well to consider the extra saving that may be affected by anticipating your wants, making up a freight order, and including millinery desired with other goods, and have them all shipped together by freight.

No. 23460 A new and very swell "Made Hat." Straw crown, wire rim covered with pleated chiffon, trimmed with ribbon loops and a beautiful steel buckle, has two tips and a bunch of "American Beauties," turned up slightly in back, finish with foliage. The cut shows one of the most stylish hats shown this year, very handsome and well worth double as much as we sell it for. Comes in black, tan and navy blue. Each......$6.95

$1.95 Buys a $3.25 Hat.

The Evette.

23465 A Regular $3.25 Trimmed Hat for $1.95. Economical Lovers of Stylish Hats Save just $1.30 when they buy this hat.

This hat is made of a fancy rough straw and is trimmed with a ruffle of ribbon and lace around crown and band of jet, loop of lace and plume on side, finished with large rosette of lace, turned up in back and finished with rosette of ribbon. People wanting a fine hat cheap, should order this hat; it is a bargain rarely seen. Each... $1.95

The Florence.

No. 23461 A $2.50 Trimmed Hat for $1.25. Milliners say these hats ought to sell for $2.50; we say $1.25 buys them. A beautiful rough straw turban, with a hair braid crown, with fold ribbon and velvet around crown; trimmed with 3 quills and fancy rosettes of ribbon and knots of velvet; very pretty twist of ribbon on right side. This is a swell hat at a very low price. Take advantage of this great bargain while you can. Colors, black, brown and navy. Price, each $1.25

A $3.50 Trimmed Hat for $2.20.

No. 23467 A hat that makes friends for our Millinery Department. Save $1.30 if you value money. A swell made hat, straw crown, wire rim, covered with lace finished with straw braid, has a beautiful ruffle of lace around crown, band of ribbon and fancy buckle in front, trimmed on right side with a very pretty plume and on left with loops of satin ribbon and bunch of violets, turned up in back and finished with large bunch of violets. Colors cream and black. Our very special price. Each.............. .$2.20

23463 The Illustration Shows a "Bon Ton" Hat that will be seen much on the fashionable boulevards of our chiefs cities this summer. Hair braids, Milan edge straw shape, trimmed with a pretty silk net in beautiful contrasting colors, one handsome plume, two bunches of roses also two pretty stick pins, turned up in back and finished with very full rosettes of silk net. Everybody that sees this hat pronounces it the "sweetest ever

Our $1.99 Leader.

No. 23469 A style made Hat, one of the lovely productions of '97. Wire frames entirely covered with handsome lace, finished with a jet edge and a very pretty jet crown, trimmed on right side with loops of lace and on left side with a handsome bunch of flowers and loops of wired lace band underneath of pleated ribbon, finished with two fancy buckles. Colors black and

Both these influences can be seen in the hats. Balancing the wide shoulders, the hats, set straight on the head, are either provided with rising trimming in Tudor styles, or if bonnet-style, have the brim tapering to a raised oval above the forehead. The only exceptions were those made by Liberty, the artistic dress warehouse established at 105 Regent Street, London, in 1884. Their hats were muted in tone, and soft in outline, appealing to the many who wanted "alternative fashion." They wanted it "hygienic," by which they meant comfortable and non-restrictive, and "esthetic," not bright or brash. Many of their modes are inspired by a remote medieval past, not the best period for comfortable hats. In retrospect, their most influential designer was not E. A. Godwin, architect and theater designer, head of the historic dress department, but Kate Greenaway, whose charming sketches of Regency children revived straw poke bonnets and soft "tams" as fashion statements.

Those for the mass market featured by Sears bear comparison for style with the charming Paris confections sketched by artists of the quality of Frederick Sandoz, in the American *Harpers Bazaar*, and the English *Queen* magazine provided fashion guidance. Sears were diffident in claiming French pedigrees for their hats; after all Paris, France, as opposed to Paris, Texas, was the last stop before perdition, as far as the Bible Belt was concerned, and in any case France was not the only source. There was a flourishing export trade in hats trimmed and untrimmed from England as well as Austria and Germany. Sears claim in 1897 that their hats "are patterned after the latest novelties from Europe. Our buyers have been unusually fortunate in securing our goods from the leading manufacturers at home and abroad . . . the large quantity ordered has lowered the price to half that of the local retail store . . . and despite the difficulty plain black and white drawings give a fair idea of the new beauty of these hat creations."

The product must have been popular, and by 1902, three times as many models were being shown, and Sears, Roebuck, growing in self-confidence, advertised "nobby," "swell" hats, "made especially for us from original designs," and the most expensive at "$5.75 . . . well worth $10" is "Genuine Paris style." It had the wide swooping shape which had become fashionable as the fashion line changed to the sinuous S-bend curve after 1900. It was "a Gainsborough effect dress hat, a very elegant hat for stylish dressers." In black and white, it had a spangled semi-tam crown and was trimmed with black velvet ribbon, an "Amazon real ostrich plume" and six black satin roses. By 1905, they also patronized the smart New York milliners, Mesdames Frances, Leman and Rentau. Italian, Leghorn straw was still a feature and Japanese imports, ribbons and straws, were beginning to be used.

The range also broadened to include sports hats, especially the sailor. This had begun to be fashionable in England in the 1870s. It was a straw with a straight-sided, shallow crown, much smaller than the mid-century sailor hats, which in accordance with the naval styles of the period, had wide upcurving brims, and a plain ribbon trim. This type of hat, made from machine-stitched straw braid, with a hard-wearing varnish finish, had reestablished the prosperity of the English Midland straw hat trade. The hats were largely manufactured in St. Albans and the trade was centred in Luton, Bedfordshire, from where the hats were exported worldwide. From the 1870s English industry had begun to use cheaper imported braid from China, and by the 1880s also from Japan, rather than locally made straw plait. The United States was also buying either imported braid or hats and by 1902, the skimmer, as it was also known, was termed the Canton Sailor in the Sears catalog.

Making the hats up became quicker when a new type of sewing machine was developed in the United States and was soon exported. When it was introduced,

Above: Yachting dress from the *Queen*, 1889, by Everard Hopkins. The group wears three types of nautical hat: the little boy an old-type sailor hat; the girls a straw sailor and a peaked yachting or "engineer's" cap.

Right: Suzanne Avril, the French musical comedy star, posed for *Les Modes* in 1901. Hat, outfit and figure all manifest the fashionable S-bend silhouette.

it was known to the English as the "10 guinea." It became the 17 guinea machine as time went on and is still used. It is not in current production, and the machines, carefully cannibalized, are factory heirlooms.

After stitching and blocking, the hats were collected from small factories and workshops into a central warehouse. Alternatively they were commissioned by the London wholesalers for home or export distribution or, increasingly, direct by the department stores to obtain a quick, cheap exclusive.

The trade was quite convinced that the vogue for boaters had begun with a new all-class interest in outdoor sports, but during the next thirty years the boater was to take residence in the wardrobes of men and women of all classes throughout the Western world. It was very popular with women, from Gibson girl to governess. Straw hats were worn with the sporty outfits that were becoming customary informal wear. During the winter they were replaced with the cloth cap. In the United States the style was retained mainly for sports, but in England, it gradually became the uniform of the unskilled working woman. Replacing the often battered bonnet, it seems almost a unisex symbol, defiant and depressed.

In England, mail order was mainly for the credit customers. For those who merely wanted a pretty hat there was the compromise between the professional milliner and home sewing. J.R. Simms in *Living London* (1902), after taking his readers on a visit to a Bond Street Modiste, Messrs. Swagger and Swell, introduced them to the small city milliner where for shillings rather than pounds you could get much the same service, a unique model. The customer chose the shape and provided the trimmings were bought at the same time, a resident milliner trimmed it up on the spot.

Everywhere the inspiration was Parisian. The well-dressed and wealthy had been making regular shopping expeditions to Paris by carriage and sailing ship even before the days of Rose Bertin, and in the 19th century, railway train and steamship, and even Cook's tour, made travel easier and cheaper. By mid-century, international exhibitions, the ultimate in trade fairs, had made the charms and resources of Paris more widely known. French success in the luxury and fashion sections were predictable and invariable from 1851. The aristocratic dream world of Louis XIV and Versailles was still a potent commercial draw.

The Paris couture dressmakers and the media began their mutual admiration campaign. Fashion bulletins, featuring M. Worth's decision to abolish the *Bavolet* from the bonnet or to introduce the Princess line in the 1870s with full cooperation from actresses, fashion artists, photographers and magazine publishers, flowed around the world. A mass market had not time to appreciate the calculated indiscretions of society gossips on which Rose Bertin, Beaulieu and Leroy had depended for publicity a hundred years before.

Even though the Modistes, the Paris milliners, never had the publicity given to the rest of the couture and always played a subordinate role in the press fashion

Below left: Country, casino and travel dress for 1895, as drawn by F. Sandoz for the *Queen* magazine. The casino outfit, (middle), the most formal, includes a small bonnet-type hat. The others seem too elaborate to be completely practical.

Below: Hats from the Sears, Roebuck catalog of 1908 are wide and heavily trimmed, perching on puffed-out coiffures. Despite their elaboration, they are intended for a popular market and are modestly priced.

Above: Parisian high fashion, 1905, in *Paquin à 5 heures* by Henri Gervex. The hats, much flowered and befeathered, are worn high on the puffed-out hairstyles, balanced on bandeaux and secured with hat pins.

features, their names soon became well known. The wealthy, beautiful and well-dressed Mrs. Augustus Newland Eddy, née Abbie Louis Spencer (1850–1909) of Chicago, was one of the ladies featured in the Chicago Historical Society exhibition *Eight Chicago Women and their Fashions 1860–1929* (1978). Advising a fellow Chicagoan, Mrs. John Jacob Glessner, before her first visit to Paris, she suggests for dresses, not Worth but Pingat and Doucet and "for hats and bonnets Virot Caroline Rebous (sic) Nevee." She was discriminating; Caroline Reboux of the rue Saint-Honoré had begun to make hats for the Empress Eugénie in 1868, and Maison Virot's models were the darlings of the smart set in the fictional pages of Ouida and Edith Wharton and can be seen in many fashion plates especially of outfits from the house of Worth. An increasing number of couture hats survive from this period. There is an excellent collection in the Costume Institute of the Metropolitan Museum of Art in New York, which includes many made for New York socialites, and the Paris Musée de la Mode has mounted two exhibitions of hats, *Les Accessoires de la Mode* (1978), and *Les Chapeaux* (1980). The notable collection of the Centre de Documentation de Costume display is scheduled for 1991.

In *Les Coulisses de la Mode* (1889) M. Coffignon put the French industry in its economic perspective. In Paris alone it employed 8000 women and each year earned 25 million francs. In addition it stimulated and provided outlets for silks from Lyons, ribbons, velvet and passementerie from Saint Etienne, laces from Calais, mounting material from Picardy, in total a trade worth 250 million francs a year.

The straw and felt shapes, the artificial flowers, the feathers and paste trimming came from Paris as indeed they still do. The designer London hat-makers depended on regular trips to Paris, and visits to the small craftsmen who had generations of experience in the confection of these inimitable and essential novelties. Those, such as buyers from the United States, who could not visit frequently, used a system of Commissionaires, collecting items to show to the buyers when they came. Lilly Daché and Alfred Solomon, founder of Madcaps, whose reminiscences are on file at the Fashion Institute of Technology in New York, remembered them cycling from the hotels with big boxes of trimmings on their backs. Indeed, bicycles apart, the world of 1880s millinery fashion has much in common with Paris now.

The Paris milliners of the 1880s were the sources of models for both the wholesale and retail trade. Many millinery firms were known merely by the first name of the owner, as this was the name by which she had been known to her clients in her previous place of business. However, M. Coffignon noted that the most creative ones preferred a private clientele because they saw a successful hat as a collaboration between designer and customer. Actresses, demimondaines with a flare for publicity and someone else to pay the bills, were their most prized clients! Any individual cash incentives were not noted by M. Coffignon.

They designed the most original and inventive blocks themselves from wire and plaster: spartery is not mentioned although known from the 1860s. They bought and commissioned blocks from the commercial blockmakers, also a current practice, but as now, they were aware that a block commissioned was a block copied. It is milliners such as these that the department store buyers visited. In the United States, customs barriers were steadily rising and new shrewd wholesalers, such as Alfred Solomon, would appreciate the advantage of licenced copying of French models, a common couture practice which in the 1930s would be regularized by the Millinery Creators Guild.

Those who made hats in the small shops, department stores and wholesale warehouses worked under variable conditions. Charles Booth, investigating the London milliners in the 1890s, found that they had the social status of shop assistant, far above that of a factory hand. A two-year apprenticeship was usual. At the top end of the scale they might earn £80 a year and the first and second hands a third to a half that. The wages, like those of most women workers, were not at all high. On the whole, they were reasonably well treated and happy in their work, and there was an awareness of the Factory Acts even if they were not always followed.

As *The Delineator* (1897) explained, millinery was a reasonable career for a woman. It was also beginning to appeal to upper-class women prepared to be déclassé because of poor circumstances. But though the social costs were high, capital costs were low, and there was a high premium on taste and good connections. Edith Wharton's tragic Lilly Bart in *The House of Mirth* (1905) never attained the little green and white shop that her friends had hoped for her, and found sewing on sequins impossibly difficult, but others were tougher survivors. There was Lucy Wallace, who later became Lucile, the internationally famous couturière in the years preceding World War I, and wife of Sir Cosmo Duff Gordon. In *Discretions and Indiscretions* (1932) she writes: "I was told that nobody would know me if I "kept a shop." It would be bad enough for a man but for a woman it meant social ruin." Gabrielle Chanel used a rich friend's gift to set herself up in business as a milliner; both Mmes. Lanvin and Schiaparelli in the 1920s took to the fashion world to survive and provide for their children, and began by making hats.

Despite the enterprise of Worth, Paquin and Lanvin, the most significant fashion statement before World War I was made by Paul Poiret. Although primarily a couturier, his concept of design was total, embracing accessories, perfume and interior design, bringing a sunburst of color into the muted

Above: The fashionable dress formally for their stroll in Hyde Park, as illustrated in a Harrods catalog of 1911. The ladies wear new-fashioned, very wide-brimmed hats with their directoire dresses, the men top hats and frock coats.

Right: Formal fashion of 1911, as illustrated by Georges Lepape for couturier Paul Poiret. The turbans recall the exotic Orient. Comparison with conventional daytime dress confirms Poiret's revolutionary influence on fashion.

fin-de-siècle world, as well as a new concept of elegant simplicity. He was not a milliner, but the odalisque turbans that he introduced in 1908 (said to have been inspired by museum specimens in the Victoria and Albert Museum), and which crown his slim oriental cum directoire dresses, and the neat bandeaux that Mme. Poiret was to continue to wear for the rest of her life, were never again to go completely out of fashion.

Just as well-known to contemporaries were the creations of Lucile. She had establishments in London, Paris and New York and a large clientele, and was particularly popular with the stage. Her designs were colorful and flamboyant and the hat she designed for Lily Elsie in *The Merry Widow* (1907), large, in the style of the period with a dramatic sweep to the brim and luxurious panache of feathers, was copied all over the world. Even today this type is still known as the Merry Widow Hat.

There is a good selection of her designs in the Victoria and Albert Museum worn by Heather Firbank, sister of the novelist Ronald Firbank, and they illustrate all aspects of pre-World War I styling. There are tip-tilted hats of about 1908, poised on bandeaux to fit them to the head, massive toques and wide-crowned sweeping cartwheels loaded with feathers, fruit and flowers which crowned the slim, hobble-skirted directoire style of 1909–12 and which always have extra-large crowns to accommodate the puffed-out hairstyles of the period. The series also includes the witty conceits of 1912–14, medium small hats which elongated the sinuous fashion silhouette with lofty waving plumes.

It is illustrative of the way in which a well-dressed and well-connected young woman managed her wardrobe that in addition to buying her hats ready-made, she also bought shapes and trimmings which her maid made up. Many came from Woollands, a smart London shop, and Aage Thaarup, the internationally famous London milliner of the 1930s to 1950s, notes in his autobiography, *Heads and Tails* (1956), that it was their old stock, cached away in their basement on which he drew in the austere years of World War II, thirty years later.

Far left: A Paris outfit for 1912, drawn by George Barbier for *Le Journal des Modes*. **The sinuous line of the coat is continued by the angle of the wide hat with its swooping feather trim.**

Left: Fashions of 1914 by H. Vallée, for *Le Journal des Modes*. **The tall hats echo the sinuous lines of the outfit.**

THE MERRY WIDOW.

Above: The Merry Widow Hat, designed by couturière Lucile for the London production of the musical comedy of that name in 1907, was a fashionable success and much copied. It helped to promote the vogue for large, elaborately trimmed hats.

The Major of Today, writing on *Clothes and the Man* in 1900, was philosophical about the top hat which had been standard town wear since before he was born: "the silk hat gets abused regularly every year . . . people say that it is ugly, unbecoming and uncomfortable." He seems to have been rather old-fashioned, or perhaps unobservant, because he goes on to note that they are becoming increasingly popular every year. Cassell's *Household Guide* had already concluded in the late 1860s that "Little can be said in favor of our stiff, ugly and uncomfortable 'chimney pot hats' but . . . we must be contented to make the best of them . . . they will inevitably have to be replaced with others of the same pattern." They were, it concluded, "a necessary evil." It then instructs on their care and preservation, for "no article becomes shabby so quickly for want of a little care," and advises on their treatment when wet, dinged, dull, salt- or water- or grease-stained. The *Household Guide* was a very middle-class publication and these were not problems which bothered the upper classes. If the servants did not care for them, they could be valeted on the spot at a good hatters such as Locke's in St. James's or Herbert Johnson in Bond Street.

Hats in general were essential accoutrements of respectability. Robert Roberts wrote about his Salford childhood in *Ragged Schooling: Classic Slum* "a man or woman, walking along the street hatless, struck one as either 'low', wretchedly poor, just plain eccentric or even faintly obscene." While at the other end of the social scale, the city man, according to Ada S. Ballin in *The Art of Dress* (1885), wore them "both in the office as well as out, all day long as a matter of form, and almost of etiquette." They were as important an item in the United States. *The Hatters Gazette* (1900) interviewed several long-established New York hatters on their recollections of the trade in 1901. N.B. Day of the Stetson Co. remembered with satisfaction the time he had sold 700 top hats direct to the department store Geneens and cleared all at $4 apiece on the first day of sale.

Right: Typical hats for the English home and export market, as promoted for the trade by the *Hatters Gazette Diary* in 1899. The pictures were intended as advertising blocks, and the gentlemen at Sudeley Castle illustrate how closely fashions were followed.

Advertisements in Local Newspapers are much more effective if Illustrated.
IT IS ONLY NECESSARY TO QUOTE THE NUMBER.

No. 1.—ELECTRO, 2/6. No. 2.—ELECTRO, 2/. No. 3.—ELECTRO, 2/6.
No. 4.—ELECTRO, 3/-. No. 5.—ELECTRO, 2/6. No. 6.—ELECTRO, 3/-
No. 7.—ELECTRO, 2/6. No. 8.—ELECTRO, 3/-. No. 9.—ELECTRO, 2/6.
No. 10.—ELECTRO, 2/6. No. 11.—ELECTRO, 2/6. No. 12.—ELECTRO, 2/6. No. 13.—ELECTRO, 2/6.
No. 14.—ELECTRO, 2/6. No. 15.—ELECTRO, 2/6. No. 16.—ELECTRO, 2/6.

ELECTROTYPES FOR ADVERTISING PURPOSES.—CASH WITH ORDER.
"HATTERS' GAZETTE," 19, LUDGATE HILL, LONDON, E.C.

Left: Making felt hats at Battersbury's factory, Stockport, in 1911; the planking room in which the felt is worked until it is the right size, consistency and shape. The "planks" on which the men work have changed little since the 18th century.

Left: Making felt hats at Battersbury's factory, Stockport, in 1911; the soft felt finishing room. Here the hats received their final block and check. The blocks were rotated and heated by machinery. The men's informal soft felt hats can be seen on the bench in the foreground.

The Major advocated choosing the style that suited and retaining it, but fashion plates and photographs show a modulation of line profile, balance of brim and crown and width of band within the period.

To a certain extent the proportion of the man's silhouette modulated in similar fashion to that of the woman. Thus in the 1870s, the cut of the coat and trousers gave a medium bulk to the figure and the hat was of moderate height but taller than it had been in the 1860s. There was a French fashion for a very wide brim, but this was not followed in England or the United States. In the late 1870s and 1880s, suits were made tight and narrow and the hat became very high indeed, slightly concave in profile with a narrow tightly curling brim and a deep band. In the 1890s, the height decreased and the crown broadened.

Making these hats was a skilled trade. In the United States it was concentrated in New York and Philadelphia, in England in London, especially in Stockwell, and in France in Paris around the Hôtel de Ville. Like the gentlemen hatters of the fur and felt hats trades, it was highly skilled and unionized. The methods seem

Above: Edward, Prince of Wales, later Edward VII, in the 1890s, in an informal lounge suit and the Homburg hat he was to make so well known.

Above right: Sears, Roebuck aimed at nationwide coverage of the American head. In their 1897 catalog they advertised sombreros, ranch and planter hats. The J. B. Stetson hat was "as worn by the most famous scout and guide in the world," a recognizable but unendorsed portrait of Buffalo Bill.

the same in England and in France and have not changed much, even today. As described by Booth, the men are the body makers, finishers and shapers and the women are the crown sewers and trimmers.

The frame or body of the hat was several thicknesses of calico stiffened with shellac and shaped over a block with a hot iron. If a layer of cork was used instead of some of the calico, it lightened but at the same time weakened the hat. An important characteristic was the strength: it protected the head and the structure was intended to withstand considerable force, still a feature of the formal riding hat. The cover or hood was made from silk plush, French material being the finest, and no longer obtainable nowadays. After the crown was sewn to the sides, it went with the body to the finishers who fixed it with shellac, making sure that the seams at the side joined as near invisibly as possible. The hat was then reblocked, and with water and hot irons given a perfect gloss. The shaper curved and molded the brim and then the woman finisher attached lining and band.

In America, judging from the Bloomingdale's, Montgomery Ward and Sears, Roebuck catalogs, the silk hat was not considered a staple of the masculine wardrobe. Its place had been taken by the hard felt bowler, or derby as it was called in the United States. Other popular hard felts were the dunlap with high crown and straight brim, and the Knox, suitable for the younger man, with a lower crown and a curly brim. There was a similar move to more informal styling in England and France. In older societies, however, there was more time lag and even in the remote countryside, the top hat lingered for Sundays, weddings and funerals, dignified if battered.

In addition there were soft felts which were considered even more informal. Sears makes a feature of Nutria fur which was an addition to the ingredients of fur felt in the 1890s. In general they were now exclusively made from hare and rabbit skins, the beaver having long since departed from the popular market to the happy hunting ground in the sky.

Hats were now a machine-made product, at least in the initial stages of their production. The hair had been sheared from the skins with a type of band saw since the 1840s and new felting methods introduced to Britain in the 1850s from the United States vastly increased production. The hairs were blown through trunking and in carefully measured quantities came to rest on gas-warmed blocks for steaming and shaping. Only in the later stages of the process was the

Below: Formally informal and fashionable, the gentlemen guests line up for a photograph by Benjamin Stone in 1899 outside Sudeley Castle, Warwickshire, unwittingly wearing outfits suitable for the prototype hats from the *Hatters Gazette;* **the gentlemen on the first left and second right wear Homburgs, still with their traditional German shape and trimming. Others wear a bowler and a tweed deerstalker with earflaps.**

Above: The fashionable young American as outfitted by Peek Clothing Co., Syracuse, in 1906. They wear high crowned Derby hats with their voluminous traveling coats.

Above right: The young men outfitted for the holidays by the Peck Clothing Co. of Syracuse in 1906 wear informal straw hats with decorative hatbands with their square-cut lounge suits.

traditional skill of the hatter needed in more than a supervisory capacity. The largest English firm was that of Christy's, now of Stockport. They were founded in 1773 in Southwark, and by 1797 were receiving most of their hats from the firm of T. & J. Worsley in Stockport which they took over in 1826. Well able to supply the increased mid-19th-century demand for felt hats, they grew steadily until the late 1930s. Now revived and amalgamated with five other houses in the trade, they are the largest worldwide producers of felt hats. With the mechanization of the process, the progressive neurological deterioration of hatters shakes, or, taking its name from the main hatting town, the Danbury shakes, as it was known in the United States, is becoming a memory.

A very popular shape of felt hat in England and the United States was the fedora, named after Sardou's play set in the 1800s and produced in 1887. It was also called the Alpine and was a compromise between the postilion shape typical of the directoire and the tapering felt folk dress hat of Bavaria. It was a soft felt hat with a taper crown shaped with a central pinch, and was almost as popular with the ladies. The trilby, named after George du Maurier's novel and play (1887) was similar, but without the taper crown and was equally fashionable in England.

For the more formal, older man, there was the homburg, introduced by Edward, Prince of Wales, and named after his favorite holiday venue, the spa of Homburg in Prussia. It was a hard hat, styled like a soft felt with a medium low crown with central pinch and a fairly wide bound and curved brim. Edward wore it with a tiny flourish of feathers at the side, emphasizing the German origin. It had a look of sly good humor, raffish yet respectable. A popular compromise between the formal and the informal, it remained in the masculine wardrobe and was the habitual wear of Anthony Eden, British foreign secretary and prime minister between the 1930s and 1950s, and was worn by General Eisenhower at his presidential inauguration in 1957.

The soft felts had increased in number and type by the end of the 19th century. In the United States the generic term "crusher" explains their advantage. They were a successful blend of the very informal town and country hat. They were joined by the telescope hat which had a circular depression in the crown, making it the forerunner of the pork-pie hat of the 1940s. The felt and felt hat industries were by now completely factory-based. But it was in the wide-brimmed felts that the United States excelled. There were a multitude of American cousins of the wideawake of England, some more or less modeled after the roughrider hat, popularized after the Spanish-American War and even more by the American cowboy hat which owed much to the Mexican sombrero. This was soon familiar to anyone who could visit the bioscope, the precursor of the cinema. The long-established U.S. firm of J.B. Stetson which produced a varied selection of good quality hats has given its name to the type as a whole.

The hot dry summers made straw hats a staple of the man's outfitting market. It was the aim of the trade to persuade every man into purchasing a new hat at the

Below: A group of Whitby fisherfolk, photographed by Frank Sutcliff in the early 20th century. The women wear four generations of the working woman's headgear. From right to left, the utilitarian and timeless kerchief; a semi-fashionable and shady hat; a man's or masculine-styled sports peaked cap; a sunbonnet deriving from those worn at the end of the 18th century. The man's peaked cap recalls the flat caps of the artisan of the 16th century.

beginning of every summer. Styles and straws were varied and the wide-brimmed planter had a long history. Panama hats, woven and not braided from the fine fibers of the Jipijapa palm and imported in bulk from South America, were quite common in the United States but expensive and cherished rarities in Europe, prized for their lightness and flexibility. In England, the hard straw boater was always more popular, partly no doubt because of its water-resistant varnished finish, though it always had an international appeal for the young smart set.

As leisure pursuits gradually became more available, sports caps increased in popularity. Generally made from fabric, they are characterized by peaks and sometimes protective flaps. The deerstalker is inalienably associated with Sir Arthur Conan Doyle's fictional detective, Sherlock Holmes. In Europe they seem to have served the same function as the American crusher, and were worn generally for comfort especially in drafty trains and soon in automobiles.

Another type of soft cap was gaining popularity, that with the one-piece crown, soft and floppy with a peak. Very popular for golf and in the car, its vogue was becoming predominantly working class, though all men probably had one in their wardrobe. It was workshop made, often under nonunionized conditions and, as a branch of the needle trades, seems to have been a speciality of the Jewish immigrant in England, France and the United States since its introduction as early as the 1830s. In England, the largest London firm, Messrs. F. Schneider & Sons, were making 4000 dozen a week by about 1900, catering both for British and world demand, and had a large export trade, particularly to the British Empire, South Africa, Australia and New Zealand, all profitable markets for the English clothing trades.

But in 1914 Europe went to war, followed soon by the United States, and the hat-makers were overwhelmed with orders for military, rather than civilian headgear. An officer leaving British service is said to be "bowler hatted" but the return to traditional headgear, at least for most men and some women, was not to take place until 1918.

WEDDING HEADDRESS

Tradition and fashion are linked with the bridal headdress. Its origin was the garland which in classical and Pauline tradition crowned the flowing locks of the virgin bride before she veiled and concealed herself as lawful wedded wife.

The wreaths were floral or jeweled, and even in the 16th century could be borrowed or hired. In 1540, St. Margaret's Church Westminster spent £3-10-0 for a "cerclett to marry maidens in."

Fashionable but not specifically bridal headdress was worn in the 17th and 18th centuries. However A.M. Earle in *Two Centuries of Costume in America 1620–1820* (1903) referred to a Pennsylvania Quaker bride with an interesting variant. When Rachael Budd married Isaac Collins at the Bank Meeting in May 1771, she wore a fashionable blue silk dress and a "black mode (silk) hood lined with white silk, the large cape extending over her shoulders." The hood, Mrs. Earle believed, was a local wedding custom mentioned in other 18th-century Philadelphia sources and may have been a German tradition.

In the early 19th century, the wreath reappeared especially with the formal wedding dress. The veil also began to be worn though the models were fashionably classical rather than modestly Pauline. The first Mrs. Earle noticed in American sources dated from about 1800, earlier than English examples, which are mainly from after 1810.

The flowers chosen for the wreath played their part in wedding folklore. The rose, the flower of Venus, was popular and also myrtle, a symbol of love. By the 1830s, the orange blossom was added, evergreen and expressive of fertility. When Queen Victoria wore a wreath of orange blossom and a veil of Honiton lace for her wedding to Prince Albert in 1840, a fashion was set for the next hundred years. The jeweled circlet seems to have been a European tradition, and came into fashion via the theater and cinema.

Wedding fashion and the whole social fabric changed in the 1960s. In the *London Daily Mail* for 15 October, 1971, a wedding expert was quoted as saying that orange blossom had begun to disappear and that brides had "moved on to one artificial rose stuck on top of 6 yards of tulle, what we call 'the miner's lamp' in the business." It was followed by space helmets à la Pierre Cardin and sou'westers from Balenciaga.

Although the tradition is modified each time a figure catches the public eye such as Princess Diana in 1981 and "Fergie," the Duchess of York, in 1986, it is also restated, and the garland and veil seem to have established themselves as classics of Western costume rather than items of fashion.

Left: Two wedding headdresses illustrated in *La Mode Illustrée*, 1872.

HATPINS

Hatpins are necessary when the hat will not balance securely on the hairstyle, or as a final decorative touch.

They were introduced at the end of the 19th century when the hats were perched on the crown or bonnets on the back of the head and may have started life early in the 19th century as decorative hairpins, the term by which they are still known in the Bloomingdale's catalog of 1887. They seem to have been about 5 inches (12.5 centimetres) long and to have been sold singly. They were popularized by Alexandra, Princess of Wales, and by the 1890s, according to the *Ladies Journal*, were becoming something of a fashion feature designed in "silver, gold or pearl and very often richly jeweled, others . . . cut jet, garnets, oxydised silver, gold Prince of Wales feathers in mother of pearl lined with gold, a Japanese fan of turquoise blue enamel, an ivory figure with spray of frosted gold, a crescent in moonstones with engraved flowers." By the turn of the century they were being made in pairs and there are some rich and charming examples in the Art Nouveau style especially by Tiffany and Lalique. They are now a popular collector's item.

As hat styles changed, some were made in sets with detachable heads and pins of different lengths, from 5 to 11 inches (13 to 28 centimetres), so that they could be adjusted to the size of the hat, for the early 20th-century hat was getting much larger, and even more insecure, supported on the bouffant Edwardian coiffure. It reached its greatest diameter in about 1911.

An 11-inch hatpin makes a very useful stiletto in the world outside the fashionable salons, and the first cries of anguish were heard in 1913, when the style of hat had changed. It, but not the hatpin had shrunk. In spring 1913, a letter to the *New York Times* told the sad story of a young man scarred for life and off work for two weeks because of an accidental jab from the two spare inches of hatpin while travelling on the Brooklyn elevated train.

But the problem was worldwide. Jabbed cheeks, even pierced eyeballs were reported from England, France and Germany. Germany was first to take action and Police President von Jagow threatened ladies with fines or imprisonment if they did not immediately fix safety finials on the end of their hatpins. There was a rush to buy "Jagow nibs" as they were called. In France, England and the United States, the ladies were slower to respond to suggestions. Indeed in both New Jersey and New Orleans, the police were called out to regulate the matter. Ladies were even charged in New Orleans, though, the embarrassed police insisted, "in a very polite manner . . . it's no joke to watch for those shining points and then approach the owners and warn them."

But by summer 1914, it was cold steel on the battlefield which was the more formidable problem and in any case styles had changed.

The twentieth century

The nations that went to war in 1914 were all convinced of the imminence of a swift and glorious victory. There followed four tragic and traumatic years. When two decades later war clouds broke again over Europe, the nations drew on hard-won experience. The 1914–18 war seems to have been the only one not followed by a rash of military styling, and in the 45 years of comparative peace which have so far followed World War II, military styles have appeared infrequently and only for particular groups. Total war takes time to forget.

The clothes in which the ladies waved the soldiers goodbye in 1914 were slim-cut and draped, topped by small neat hats with upstanding trimming. To those who remembered the massive mountains of luxurious trimmings and the soft mounds of hair, characteristic of directoire styling, they lacked charm: "rammed on the head always at an angle," we are told and "singularly ugly, the hard line round the brow."

By the end of the first year of war, the fashion silhouette had begun to change,

Below: The fashions shown at the International Exhibition, Chicago, 1915, in an illustration for the *Gazette du Bon Ton* by Georges Lepape. The upstanding slanting trimming on the new-fashion small hats balances the almost crinoline line of the shorter skirts.

Right: Fashions for 1922 by Patou, from *Art Goût Beauté.* On the left and right, alternative hats are shown with the same outfit to be seen with and without its jacket: a broad-brimmed straw and a ruche-trimmed beret. In the middle, with the sports outfit, is a close-fitting cap with a spiky feather trim.

confirming women's new status as useful members of the workforce. Shorter and wider skirts were more convenient and to balance a wider, more down-to-earth line, the hats lost some of their vertical emphasis, but began to be worn at a dramatic angle, enhanced by spiky sideways trim. The fashionable hat is far more aggressive than the simple rather sporty felts allocated to some of the women working at men's jobs.

Factory workers were given mob-caps, like those worn by maidservants for rough work, mainly as protective headgear, since long hair was dangerous and hairpins were soon going to be difficult to find. In mute reaction, freedom for some women would soon mean the right not to wear a hat. The short hairstyles of the 1920s and the hatless vogue can be seen in relation to wartime conditions.

It was not until 1920–21 that the fashion direction was established, confirming, at least the straight and simple and the low waistline. In the immediate postwar period, it had dallied with alternatives, high versus low waists, drapes, hip puffs and a miscellaneous folk inspiration, a belated return to Poiret's prewar exoticism.

The hats were mainly toques and cloches, a shape which Gabrielle Chanel is said to have introduced in her prewar career as a milliner. The term cloche was originally used for a hat with a bell-shaped crown but soon became almost generic for the hat we associate with the 1920s, fitting the head so closely it seemed to be molded to the skull, giving the lady a streamlined appearance, likened to a Brancusi bird.

Materials, textures and colors varied as did decorations but the unifying feature was the angle, or lack of it: hats were worn straight and pulled low over the forehead. To Edna Woolman Chase, editor in chief of *Vogue* during the period, "chic started at the eyebrows" and Loelia, Duchess of Westminster was almost reduced to recognizing her friends by their teeth. The trimmings were restrained, conforming to and not distracting from the shape. There was a vogue for attaching a gleaming ornament to front or side, which if the jewel were real, could cause problems if the hat were left in a cloakroom. In most cases the trimming was just a plastic clip, Art Deco in style, a tiny tuft of flowers or feathers or a small bunch of fruit.

To enhance these subtle shapes, milliners evolved and refined their techniques. The fashionable hairstyle was cut close to the head, bobbed or shingled. Hats had to fit because there was nothing here to grip a hat pin. Sizing was important, as was molding to the shape of the head. The relationship of smart woman and milliner was almost intimate, and the hats were twisted, molded and tucked to size and shape enhancing the essential style of each client. Caroline Reboux, Maria Guy, Agnès and Rose Valois had a reputation for understated enhancement. For those who wanted something less austere, there was the toque, with its looser crown and more varied, softer arrangement.

M.D.C. Crawford, editor of *Woman's Wear Daily*, knew the ladies concerned and his thumbnail sketches in *The Ways of Fashion* (1941) cannot be improved: "Reboux, like Vionnet, excelled in line and modelled simplicity and avoided, as far as possible the use of ornament. Her great vogue was in the 1920s and into her old fashioned and rather dingy salon crowded the smart women of the world." The designer was Mme. Lucienne. He recalls Mme. Agnès as the best-known designer to come from Reboux, setting up on her own in 1917, soon moving opposite to smart couturier of the period Jean Patou. Although she worked with the same discrimination as Reboux, she had immense awareness of the artistic trends of the 1920s, and is said to have brought Jean Dunand, master of eggshell lacquer, into the fashion sphere. He made many of her ornaments.

By the later 1920s the line had begun to change, the skirt to lengthen from its mid-1920s heights, flare and droop at the side or back. In sympathy the hat line also began to modify, leaving more of the forehead bare and sometimes

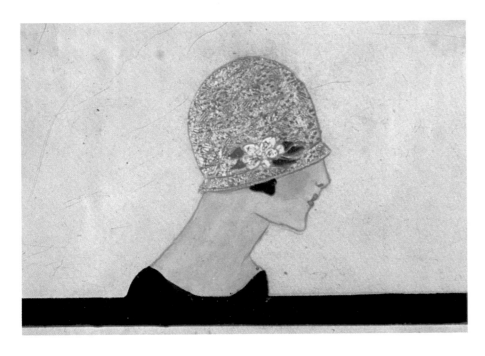

Left: A cloche hat of 1926, designed by Jeanne Lanvin. It illustrates the fashion at its most demanding, pulled so far down that it conceals the eyes.

Above: Clara Bow promotes hats for Sears, Roebuck in 1927. Youthful and popular, they are less dramatic and difficult to wear than the high fashion hats.

Above right: The hats of the early 1930s are asymmetric, complementing the bias-cut grace of the dresses.

developing an asymmetric flare. In 1927, a "one-eyed hat" was introduced worn "tilted ever so little to the back and just a thought sideways," and by 1928, some had the front brim turned up, revealing the plucked eyebrows so long concealed. At the end of the decade, the hat framed rather than concealed the face, balancing a fashion line which had also decisively changed, with the waist at an almost natural level and a longer and fuller skirt.

An alternative to the cloche, especially for summer or semiformal wear at the races or at garden parties, was the picture hat for those who craved traditional romance and not the brusque rejection of sentiment alleged to be typical of the cloche-wearing flapper. The wide, often semitransparent brim was sometimes combined with a contrast-textured, draped crown, soft floating feathers and ribbons. Caroline Reboux made many hats for couturière Madeleine Vionnet's clients, and they harmonize beautifully with the soft floating line: picturesque, but never overloaded with trimmings.

For evening wear, bandeaux or neat turbans replaced hats, the brow enhanced with jewels or feathers. By the 1920s, film stars were the creatures of contemporary mythology and their styles, especially the romantic and the picturesque were avidly followed. Realizing this, joint trade and cinema promotions became commonplace. The elegant Gloria Swanson could always be relied on to promote a fashion and it was well-known that she dictated her own styles and was not one to be bullied by Paris designers. Clara Bow, the "It girl," a star whose lack of dress sense was the despair of designer Travis Banton, makes a smiling appearance in the Sears, Roebuck catalog of 1927, modeling "Misses and Young Women's hats." Conforming to screen rather than fashionable convention, and dictated by film lighting, they are worn well off the face and clear of the eyes.

Greta Garbo was less obliging offscreen but her example launched the sporty Basque beret so effectively it has repeatedly returned to fashion, and her fashion flare on set was designer Adrian's delight. In Sweden, before entering films, she had been a millinery assistant and model, and the skill never left her. She was to promote some of the most romantic styles of the early 1930s, and with the off-the-face hats which had become fashionable, there was no longer need for compromise between screen and street style. The tip-tilted Eugénie hat in 1860s mode which she wore in *Romance* in 1930, the sweeping cavalier brims from *Queen Christina* (1933), the high Victorian of *Anna Karenina* (1935) and *Camille* (1936), all helped the woman in the street to appreciate the charisma of the past.

This important element was brought up to World War II when New York milliner Mr. John designed demure bonnets, dashing tip-tilted pork-pies for Walter Plunkett's costumes in *Gone with the Wind* (1940), bringing an important element of romance into war-time styling. It was only one among the many films he dressed, bringing fashion into the lives of the millions.

The decorative importance of the hat in the wardrobe increased as the line of fashion changed. In the early 1930s the clothes had been slinky and bias cut, echoed by the small close-fitting hats with their marked diagonal movement. But by the middle of the 1930s there was a noticeable rise in the line of the waist and the breadth of the shoulders. It gave a rather chunky look which was redeemed by the wit and charm of the hats poised high on the head. Hairstyles, close-set waves, sleekness of curls, were important and in the most successful examples, hair and hat form a unified three-dimensional creation.

In the hands of Madame Schiaparelli, one of the best-known couture designers of the decade, this aspect was fully exploited: she had trained as a sculptor before

Above left: Hats in 1930 had begun to be worn farther back from the face. Illustrated in *Art Goût Beauté*, September 1930, were, from left to right, a grosgrain hat by Maria Guy, a Jane Blanchot in black velvet and another trimmed with appliquéd feathers; a Le Monnier in velvet and crin (horsehair braid).

Above: Basic yet smart styling in 1931. The useful plain, neat, head-hugging hats complement the slim fashionable line.

Above: A knitted hat designed and here worn by Elsa Schiaparelli, 1932. Sportswear and knitted fashions were her most popular early designs. A simple cap like this would soon have been copied for the popular market.

Above right: A neat yet witty hat by Elsa Schiaparelli, photographed by the late Cecil Beaton in 1936. The joky quality of the design, a feature of millinery fashion of the late 1930s, is emphasized by the photograph.

opening her establishment in 1928, and was always sensitive to artistic influences. Well conceived in fashionable terms, her clothes had another dimension; they were topical, allusive and witty, talking points in smart society. Her design career had begun in sportswear and her Madcap, her first success, was one that Alfred Solomon remembered as a successful launch on the transatlantic market, purchased as quickly as he could get them crocheted. Actress Ina Claire modeled her simple all-adaptable knitted cap with equal success. Other models were more recherché. There was the Shoe Hat of 1937, of surrealist inspiration. Madame Schiaparelli herself and fashion leader and *Harpers Bazaar* editor Daisy Fellowes are said to have been the only two daring enough to wear it. It is a soft, light, forward-tilted beret with a graceful peak simulating the heel of the shoe at the back. There is an example in the Costume Institute of the Metropolitan Museum of Art in New York. Her theme collections inspired many models. From the Circus collection of 1937 came clown hats, tapering cones; and ringmasters' hats, sleek chimney pots. This zany eclectic attitude to design was shared with designers in New York and London.

Lilly Daché of New York, Paris-trained at Caroline Reboux and Suzanne Talbot, opened her first tiny New York atelier in 1926 and progressed to make 9000 hats a year by 1965, when she closed. In her autobiography *Talking Through My Hats*, she tells how she became the first New York milliner to make hats front-page news. Her contacts with Hollywood were close, and working with Travis Banton, she designed the draped toques with which Marlene Dietrich made such an impression in *Desire* (1938). For the Brazilian Bombshell, Carmen Miranda, there were the towering turbans loaded with fruit and flowers which managed to both satirize and provide models for early 1940s fashions. At the other extreme she made the simple half hat which was worn by prewar New York debutante Brenda Frazier. Popularized with a snood by Betty Grable, it launched millinery on the mass fashion market at the beginning of World War II. Less successful was the attempt with two friendly rivals, Mr. John and Sally Victor in the Joint Designer Group, to try and establish unified direction among the welter of styles for the wholesale millinery trade. There were just too many ideas. Crazy nonsense hats were front-page news on the eve of World War II.

Above left: High fashion hat designed by Eric and illustrated in *Les Modes*, 1936. The hats of the late 1930s could be witty and fantastic. Eric's work was well known through the 1940s and 1950s.

Above: Aage Thaarup designed this hat for Elizabeth, the Queen Mother, for her tour of South Africa in 1947, making use of ostrich feathers, a local product. It conformed to her taste for light, pretty styles, and the feathers gave added height. It has become a royal classic and may be compared with John Boyd's hats for Princess Diana in the early 1980s.

Left: Ladies' hats for all types and all U.S. occasions as advertised by Sears, Roebuck in 1938.

London also had its star milliner, Danish-born Aage Thaarup, who came to England in 1932 by way of Berlin, Paris and India where he made his first English upper-class clients who were to stay with him for the rest of his professional career. He told his story in *Heads and Tails* (1956). He was a success from the first photographs of one of his models as worn by Lili Damita, and photographed by Cecil Beaton for *Vogue*. He shared with Mr. John a Puckish charm and a genuine sensitivity to a woman's desire to protect and project her personality through her hat, as well as have it given a form which would enhance the outfit as a whole. His customers soon included international socialites like Thelma, Lady Furness, for whom, he writes, he introduced the halo hat, and Mrs. Simpson, later Duchess of Windsor. He demonstrated his talent for the exotic with the burnous drape that he designed for Marlene Dietrich and coolie hats for Anna May Wong in *Chu Chin Chow*. Like Schiaparelli, he espoused the bizarre, and his surrealist show in the late 1930s was very successful.

He made many hats for the English royal family including the Duchess of York, later Queen Elizabeth and now the Queen Mother, and which culminated in the models for the royal tour of South Africa in 1946 and the coronation festivities of Queen Elizabeth II.

The gloom and shortages of World War II provoked rather than deterred him, and his miniature-hat "Gift Tokens" were a charming inspiration. But despite the enthusiasm aroused by his many tours round the country materials were in very short supply and hats, the prices of which were not controled, became very expensive. Convinced that despite all difficulties "women were looking for a bit of magic," he became, after the war, the first couture milliner to design for the wholesale trade, collaborating with the hat manufacturers in Luton to make first his Teen and Twenty range.

His awareness of the philosophy and psychology of the hat-wearing woman is shown in *Pinpoints*, a magazine he sponsored and which he designed with friends in 1938. The first number includes an article by Tom Harrisson, pioneer journalist of *Mass Observation* and popular British magazine *Picture Post* fame. In semi-serious vein, Harrisson compares the hat-wearing habits of the "smart socialist" in East London and the "smart socialite" in Mayfair, and concludes that there was not much difference in their hat-buying habits. Both observed the two main hat seasons, spring and fall, and in the more prosperous working-class district, the women below 40 bought between three and four, and those over 40 two or three hats a year. What he did not mention was that prices in the East End of London were about a twentieth of those in Mayfair.

From 1937, *Mass Observation*, founded by Tom Harrisson and Charles Madge Maude, was to be a prime source on the realities of life, as opposed to the dream world of the fashion magazine, the optimistic forecast of the trade or the rosy recollections of old-timers. In a regular series of surveys, now filed at the University of Sussex, England, they attempted to gather information for objective assessment.

The development of an English popular ladies' hat trade was the creation of the town of Luton in Bedfordshire which, since the 18th century had been the center of the straw hat industry. The core of their prosperity was what an employee of the firm of W. Wright, now the largest maker of hats for the retail trade, and who started work there in the early 1930s at the age of fourteen, called a "shopping hat." As Harrisson had discovered, the hat was still as necessary to a decent middle-aged woman as her shoes and her handbag. The vogue of going hatless which had developed among the sporty young in the 1920s coincident with that all-weather accessory, the automobile, was for those who were too young for or beyond convention. They would have agreed with *Mass Observation*'s comment in 1939: "Increasing hatlessness has gone along with churchlessness. The church for centuries has made women feel that without a hat they were unsuited for the sight of God or of any other strange man."

The hoods, the basic shapes, were brought into the main factory from the many smaller workshops or were imported from central Europe, especially Germany and Austria. Colors were limited to black, brown and navy blue, though light-colored felts were introduced on the eve of World War II. They were a problem to make up, and far too easy to get finger- or machine-stained. The blocking was done in the factory and trimming either there or as home work. It seems that the factory was not unionized. It was a small family firm and the women found that piecework was more profitable.

The designs could come from any source: the cinema; a walk round the West End shops (time off allowed); a tip-off from a blockmaker. On the eve of war, business was booming and they were employing their first designer.

The demands of total war took immediate effect in England as they did in the United States when it entered the war in 1941. Germany had to a large extent already cut back on consumer goods and was making increasing use of synthetics.

In England the output of hats was controled at two-thirds its prewar level. The work force was depleted, there were service demands to be met and the Purchase Tax raised the price. Materials were immediately affected and *Mass Observation* noted that by December 1940, Britain was short of 750,000 hoods from Italy and Japan. Exports from central Europe, either hoods (many made from jute mixtures), and passementerie trimmings from Czechoslovakia were also cut off.

Government propaganda and the press picture of the war years is one of determined make do and mend, the aim an illusion of normalcy and sex appeal as

Left: Utility outfits designed by Norman Hartnell for Berketex in 1943 show British wartime styling. The moderate-sized, essentially prewar type hats should be compared with the French wartime fashions shown on the next page.

national therapy. To *Vogue* in 1941 "it is axiomatic that the good spirits of the fighting men depend on the civilian and more particularly the female of the species. And what do hers depend on? Well largely on her clothes . . . This business of looking beautiful is largely a duty." Underlying this was the wish to retain the British fashion industry for its trade potential. Their success must be gauged by the postwar record, and its shop window, the Britain Can Make It exhibition (1946); many came to look, but none could buy.

It is the promotional side that is illustrated in the fashion journals. There was the escapist mode, jaunty tip-tilted hats, a development of the Schiaparelli Doll Hat of the late 1930s, trimmed with artificial flowers and twists of colored ribbon. On examination, they can be seen to be made of a patchwork of felt pieces. Ingenuity was the watchword, and in 1940 Ann Edward commissioned Aage Thaarup to design hats for *Picture Post* that could be made for two shillings (20p) each. In keeping with the square-shouldered, rather dumpy, look of English wartime fashion, there were many military models, but as Anne Edwards noted in December 1939: "I have visited all the fashion shows, but the moment anything military shows, people say I don't want to wear anything that looks like military caps."

Some hats were worn as a necessity. The turban, for instance, a charming prewar creation by Paris milliner Suzy, could be made from almost any spare length of fabric. Warm and protective, it was, as Cecil Beaton wrote in *Vogue* in 1942, "the emblem of practicality for Mrs. Churchill and the munitions girl." For winter it was supplemented by the Pixie Hood, a return to the medieval *capuchon*, simple and straight to make, and often knitted, as well as the net snood. Both

Below: French fashions of 1943, the styles that astonished the rest of the fashionable world. The hats dominate and yet balance the short skirt line and the clumpy shoes.

were a return to prehistoric hat basics. The royal family led by espousing the babushka, the peasant-style scarf of Russian allies, and indeed wear it as a compromise with the "no hat" mode to this day.

Inevitably, as prices rose, in some cases 400% by the end of the war, people ceased wearing hats. In a snap survey in September 1941, *Mass Observation* found that three-quarters of young people in the business area of London were not wearing them. It was a very different picture from prewar days, and hats for decency would be a principle which would never return.

It is less easy to give the United States picture because the cultural and indeed climatic picture was so diverse, but the story line is similar; artist milliners noticing a boom in pretty hats for occasions; supply shortages; the influences of films and the media which give a brilliant and seductive picture of the fashions of the time. But there were also the young growing up in a new tradition: if it was not useful, not precisely beautiful and cost a lot, why have it?

The role of Paris is ambivalent and still under assessment. For years, its milliners had been known worldwide through coverage in the glossy magazines and the forays of the American wholesale trade. Lilly Daché describes her trips to Paris as does Alfred Solomon and Elizabeth Hawes, later a New York designer, but at that stage in her life a combination style-scout and pirate.

On the eve of the German invasion, Paris hats were at their most chic and ingenious. Despite the prestige of the modistes such as Agnès, Suzy, Georgette, Rose Valois, and Rose Descat, it is probable that Schiaparelli's hats were the best known to the general public. In *In My Fashion* (1960) Bettina Ballard, *Vogue* editor leaving Paris for New York in 1939 "took no less than 20 of the most conspicuous hats in Paris " . . . I was hat mad . . . for a real shocker I took Schiaparelli's gold embroidered black monkey jacket, a long black skirt, and a matching high chechia hat." Usually becoming, they were invariably news-worthy. Balenciaga's hats were also becoming well known. He was only established in Paris from 1937, but his success was swift. The hats he showed were designed by his friend and partner Vladzio D'Attainville. During the war they acquired increasing drama and originality and impact; indeed the house narrowly escaped closure by the Germans on account of their extravagance.

Bulletins through neutral countries showed Paris hats steadily increasing in size, ingenuity and vivacity. Under the German occupation, the Paris fashion line had begun to diverge from that of England and the United States. It was more rounded and altogether bulkier. Over the almost exaggeratedly feminine shapes with neat waistlines and balancing the short hemlines rose a series of enormous arrangements, swooping pillboxes of Maginot-line proportions and flower-studded halos. The materials might range from farmyard feathers, through fabric scraps to wood shavings and old newspaper, but combined with skill, the results were dazzling, especially to those used to the more understated fashions of London and New York.

In interviews after the liberation of Paris in September 1944, the Paris couture explained their deviant design. As Bettina Ballard reported in *Vogue*, quoting Monique de Serreville, the Paris couture "represented a French industry of primordial importance . . . it was the means of avoiding unemployment for the workers." Not only was it an affirmation of normality, defiant in the circumstance of alien occupation, it was also, according to Lucien Lelong, President of the Syndicat de la Couture, a demonstration of "Fashion . . . in its most extravagant form. The modistes have made huge ridiculous hats just to spoof the Germans who took all fashion extravagance seriously . . . "

La Théâtre de la Mode show, a chic miniature representation of completely accessorized Paris couture was organized in 1945 to confirm that French fashion

Above: An outfit designed by Cristobal Balenciaga for Plaire in 1946. The hat, an extravagant flower-trimmed toque, together with the exuberant romance of the outfit, foreshadows New Look styling, which was to be launched in early 1947.

Above: A hat from the Harrods 1948 catalog. It is in the style of the 1880s, conforming to the New Look, a consciously reactionary romantic revival.

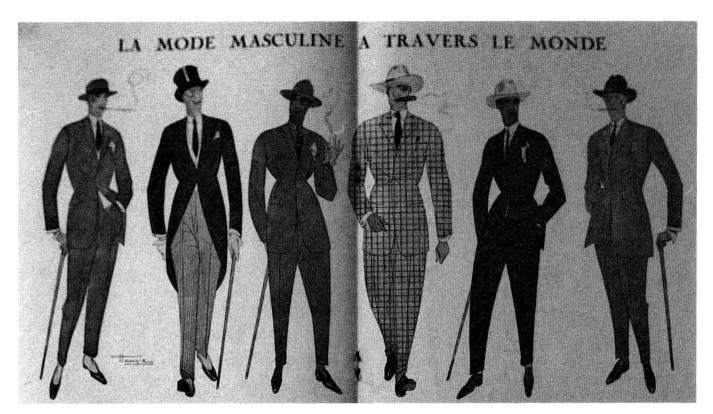

LA MODE MASCULINE A TRAVERS LE MONDE

Above: International fashion for men from *Monsieur*, 1923. There is considerable variation in the shape and balance of the informal felt hat, but the formal top hat is now fixed in style.

was still lively. It circulated around the world. Quite unexpectedly the fully dressed miniatures have been rediscovered, and after temporary exhibition in Paris and New York will return to their permanent home, the Maryhill Museum of Fine Arts, Washington, U.S.A.

In 1948, *Mass Observation* surveyed men's attitudes to wearing hats and found that the 16 to 25-year-olds in particular were disinclined to consider the conventions of prewar years. Only a third of them wore one and the proportion dropped to 13 percent in those below 25. There was the expense, and for men, hats meant uniform and authority, not a freedom for which they had been fighting. If hat they had to have, then three-quarters of them preferred a trilby, known in the United States as the snapbrim.

These findings were not surprising, because in the interwar years there had been an increasing search for informality. Their fashion leader was Edward, Prince of Wales, later and briefly, Edward VIII. As a young man he was a rebel in his dress, but he accepted with pleasure the role as an ambassador of British fashion providing that he could stress the informal and wear the comfortable. On his American visit in 1924 *Men's Wear* noted "a minor but new and correct change in the detail of men's wear" which could be credited to the Prince of Wales. He wore a snap brim, "the favorite headgear for men in the public eye for town and country comfort." But it had style as well for "it will be noticed that the brim is considerably wider and that the higher crown tapers more to a point when worn to a single center crease than the average hat." And, for those who had observed the prince's individual way with its arrangement, one could be bought from Sears, Roebuck for about $4 with the additional confirmation of its fashionability by the name "Bond Street."

The prince's informal tastes were not appreciated by his father, George V, who considered even bowlers informal country hats for "ratcatchers," and wore them in public only on the rare occasions when he appeared without a formal frock coat. His example was followed by others. The top hat was still worn in the City. For such men the informal hat was the homburg.

In America the bowler or derby had almost half a century of social respectability behind it. Its associations were with the Democratic Party, and the brown derby was linked to their nominee for the Presidency in 1919, Alfred E. Smith, governor of New York. It also gave its name to a well-known Hollywood restaurant. Clothing style was given to politics by Mayor James J. Walker of New York with his elegance and deftly poised informal hats.

At another level in society in this Prohibition era, the cinema was giving the gangsters style and charisma. It is impossible to think of them without their snap-brim borsellinos. It was at this time that the high-quality handmade hats from the long-established firm of Borsellino in Monza began to make an impact on the American market.

The line of the 1920s suit was comparatively high-waisted, the trousers were fairly wide and the shoulders were unstressed. By the mid-1930s, it had begun to be made looser with broader squarer shoulderline and a lower waistline. The whole silhouette had become chunkier.

Confirming the line, hats began to be made lower, sitting more firmly on the head. An English innovation was the pork-pie, a sports hat usually made from

Left: Everyday country hats of 1920, as worn by Mr. and Mrs. Macmillan on their honeymoon. Her hat is shady and broad-brimmed; he wears a cloth cap.

Right: Conventional men's wear in 1938, as suggested by British multiple man's tailor Montague Burton. A homburg hat is worn with the formal suit, and a trilby for informal all-weather wear.

Right: Harrods men's styling in 1948 reflects the new trend towards formality. A homburg is still advocated for semiformal wear, and the soft felt hat combines Anglo-American trends and is a combination of pork-pie and trilby.

Above: Bing Crosby in 1957, unusually formal in trilby and double-breasted suit.

rough finish felt and distinguished by a crease around the tip of the crown which made it similar to the American telescope hat, a young American style before World War I. It was to continue to be fashionable until the 1940s, its distinction coming from the precise alignment of the pinch at the front of the crown and the angle of the brim. The optimists, the Andy Hardys of the world, wore it with the brim turned up. For those for whom this style was too ingenuous, there was the Alpine hat with its tapered crown, narrow snap brim and cord band. It was textured and colored like its European counterparts but began to look worryingly Teutonic as war clouds loomed.

The interest in sports grew during the postwar years and most young men owned specialized headgear. For summer there was the boater. It had been popular for so long it was almost acceptable as a semiformal summer hat for the older man, and could certainly be worn without eccentricity in town with a lounge suit, at least in the 1920s.

Nevertheless in England, its vogue with the young must have begun to wane, because at the request of the Chairman of the Executive Council of the Textile and Allied Trades section of the British Industries Fair in 1924, the Prince of Wales agreed to wear a boater instead of going bareheaded.

By the mid-1930s, as the slump began to lose its hold, the plain panama-type hat began to lose ground before a great variety of summer straws, especially in the United States. It was becoming fashionable to dress as though you had spent your vacation on some exotic and tropical shore.

For all-year-round wear, the soft cap retained appeal, again promoted by the Prince of Wales, who wore one for golf and informal country occasions. It was particularly popular with motorists since it hugged the head, did not blow off, and was flat and warm, necessary in a time of open or unheated cars. However in England their appeal for the middle classes was compromised by their artisan overtones. They were really only admissible made in wool and worn with very good quality tweeds or sports clothes. As the slump deepened in the early 1930s it was becoming very important to be able to distinguish the man who was at leisure and the man who had no work to do.

The man in the cloth cap had become a stereotype. There were even tales that Keir Hardie, the first trade unionist to take his seat in the English parliament in 1910, had so in a cloth cap. In fact, always a comfortable careless dresser, he wore a deerstalker, his traveling hat. John Burns, a boilermaker and also an early Socialist member, habitually wore a bowler and a blue serge suit, the dress of the respectable skilled practical engineer. From 1939–1945 sartorial social distinctions were replaced by uniform. At the end of the war in Britain, the demob outfits of civilian clothes always included a hat, giving men an equal start in the Land Fit For Heroes.

In the postwar world, fashion hesitated. Peace did not mean plenty and until 1948, England was in the grip of crippling shortages, international debts as well as cold winters and sunless summers. The United States too, had its problems. Moreover, in the years of war it had gone its own fashion way and found a new easy-moving sporty simplicity of styling. This was not the atmosphere for a romantic revival and when Christian Dior of Paris introduced a revised version of the immediate prewar styles unanimously hailed as the New Look, it was greeted with appalled delight. It was the antithesis of seven years of sensible dressing with

Above: U.S. men's hats had a high tapering crown complementing their broad-shouldered suits.

Left: A drawing by Cynthia Barrell illustrates the New Look, 1947, a celebration of the return of the extravagance of high fashion after wartime austerity.

Above: A hat designed by Dior, 1956. Wide-brimmed and flower-trimmed, it was a fashionable and important accessory. Hats were worn for semiformal social occasions such as restaurant dining.

Above right: Balenciaga's designs were always dramatic and took their inspiration from varied sources. In this group from the 1940s can be seen, to the far right, a medieval inspiration; in the middle, a neat cloche, and on the far left a beret, 16th-century in style, embellished with Spanish pompons.

its cinched-in waist, drooping restrictive shoulders and a skirt too long and full for easy movement. Nevertheless it was irresistible.

With the new line, hats began to widen, balancing the width of the skirt. The hats by Sven, Albouy and Eric echo the dramatic sweeping line of the hem or diminish the importance of the head with their small neat shape. The mood was formal and the materials were often luxurious, rich melusine, softest velvet, fur and feathers.

The hats of Balenciaga take their own path. Designed in-house, they have a rare and sculptural severity. Inspired by Spanish sources, there are top hats, as worn by the herdsmen of Guetamaria, and tiny tip-tilted boaters as worn in the Canary Islands.

During the 1950s, following in Balenciaga's wake, a more sculptural form began to take over from the New Look. With the severe structured styles, accessories became very important, handbags grew larger, umbrellas longer and heels rose. The hat was just another accessory in the ensemble. At its largest, it framed the face and head and left the forehead and nape of the neck clear, enhancing the infinitely extended line of neat poised head on long neck.

In the popular market the great craze was the feathered half hat. Hairstyles were neat and close to the head, and a roomful of young girls could look like a corps de ballet. Mascara-tinged eyes and veils added to the exotic effect.

This was the great period of chain store millinery, glamorous and international in style and appeal. Russian discus-thrower Nina Ponomareva, Naughty Little Nina, as she became known to the British press, brought the international sporting world almost to a standstill in 1956 when she was charged with stealing four feather hats from C&A Modes in London's Oxford Street, and sent home in disgrace, with the Russian athletics team following in her wake.

In the early 1960s, the fashion hat had to cope with new problems. The products of the postwar baby boom were growing up and taking over fashion leadership and, on the whole, as we have seen, the young were anti-hat. Skirts became shorter, clothes were straight and simple, and style was restless and quick moving. Then, in 1964, Courrèges, followed by Cardin, sent the young into the Space Age with their new collections.

The immediate problem for the milliner was the hairstyle, bouffant, back-combed and lacquered and expensively impregnable. Makeup confirmed the spaced-out effect, matte and masklike. There was not much a hat could add, and a great deal from which it could distract.

The top designers confirmed their looks with their hats; Cardin and Courrèges, the newsmaking couturiers of the decade, introduced space-age helmets which the English milliner James Wedge translated into light wearable helmet hats. His clientele were young, pop stars and their girl friends, and his transparent hood shapes evoke an atmosphere of almost childlike innocence. Another function of the hat was to decorate the sculptural mounds of high-piled, firmly lacquered hair. Light commodious hats gave it another texture, crowning it with petals. *Vogue* noted "the hat that's a flower . . . like putting your head into an enormous chrysanthemum." Neither James Wedge nor his clients seem to have kept hats from this period, but those of another English milliner of the period, Otto Lucas, are now cherished with affection and admiration. Those who have worked with him confirm his talent as a maker of utterly becoming hats.

At the other end of the scale, it was advisable to have some chic head covering at hand to cover the hair rollers.

For the young designers Mary Quant and Barbara Hulanicki at Biba, the accent was on the hat as an irrelevance. There were Baker Boy berets and soft romantic large-brimmed pull-on felts and straws. The young were making their standards and as *Vogue* wrote: "every day and in every way you can be different and different and different." The dressing-up box look was to persist into the 1970s.

Above: A Paris suit of 1956, its elongated pencil line dramatized by the broad-brimmed hat.

Left: A hat of the 1960s, a collage fantasy designed by milliner Rudolph of London, but illustrating the fashionable puff-ball look.

**Right: A golfing cap cum
Baker Boy beret designed by
Daniel Hechter to accompany
his golfing outfit for winter
1972–73.**

Left: A Spanish hat accessorizes Jacques Esterel's Gaucho outfit for 1967. The hood gives it a timeless look, space age or medieval according to choice.

Right: 1974 and the romantic rural look, an eclectic mixture of styles with broad-brimmed felt accompanying floppy, flower-print dresses.

In the United States, despite Mary Quant's triumphant tour in 1965, this zany look was mistrusted. They had their own ideal in Jackie Kennedy, Queen of Camelot, neat, trim, and supremely elegant. She wore no hat for her husband's inauguration, but thereafter one appeared on suitable occasions. Ellen Melnikoff in *What We Wore* (1974), an off-beat special history of women's clothing, based on the recollections of American women who grew up in the period, notes: "Jackie's pill-box was the last of the serious hats. It was perky, simple and chic," and several of her informants included pillboxes in their Jackie look-alike kits, even if they did not come from Oleg Cassini.

Nevertheless, it was the beginning of the bad years for the milliner and the hatter. Jane Shilton, whose memories of the period are on file at the Fashion Institute of Technology, New York, recalls a buyer, panic-stricken at the design void, being sent by her boss to watch at a fashionable street corner and reassure herself that ordinary women were still wearing hats, for decoration, decency, and weather protection.

There was still the special occasion, the wedding and bar mitzvah trade, hats as a ritual necessity. Most were plain and set lightly on the ostentatious and expensively dressed hair. In addition to Jackie's pillbox there were Breton Sailors and Puff Ball Toques.

English style leadership came from the crown, a family with whom a large proportion of the women in the street could identify. The Queen, Elizabeth II, young, married, hard-working with a family of young children, always seemly and suitable, was dressed by Norman Hartnell, Hardy Amies and Ian Thomas, and many of her hats came from Rose Vernier and Simone Mirman, a London milliner trained in classic Paris tradition, who had worked with Schiaparelli in London after World War II. Adept at simple styling, her hats found their way into many costume collections after a Christie's sale of her lifetime collection in 1978. Since 1968, there have also been hats from Freddie Fox, a New Zealand designer and milliner, witty, urbane and perceptive, who works with Hardy Amies and Philip Somerville.

The alliance of milliner with couture house has been a long-standing practice in the fashion trade. It helps to create the total look and the consistency of line which is an essential ingredient of fashion at its most restrained and classic. A good presentation also depends on teamwork. From the designer's point of view, hats and clothes are essentially complementary and help to sell one another, important at a time when licensing and wholesale tie-ups are a financial fashion imperative. Currently a high proportion of the Paris couture houses have close links with block and hoodmakers, basic but essential in the creation of a wider market.

From press photographs of those years, the hats obey the royal imperative. They suit the Queen, who like her sister, the Princess Margaret, and Elizabeth the Queen Mother, is not tall; their hats are easy to put on, comfortable and gently stylish. Unlike the massive toques worn for so many years by her grandmother Queen Mary, they are not ritualized and timeless. In private life it seems the Queen rarely wears hats, though when protection is needed she reverts to the head scarf of her youth, a fashion also adopted by U.K. "Preppies," the Sloane Rangers.

Above all, they never conceal the face. Fashionable Princess Marina had worn a flapping picture hat in the Silver Jubilee celebrations for George V in 1936, and this had been a lesson never forgotten. Like the rest of society, the royal family shares the English high season summer vogue for hats for Ascot, garden parties and society weddings. Although their outfits are noted by the press, it is unfair for millinery as an art or craft that the press photographer often prefers to record the ostentatious attention-seeking creations.

The investiture of the Prince of Wales at Caernarvon Castle, Wales, in 1968, a ceremony which goes back to the 14th century, illustrates the royal attempt to blend the rituals of royalty with the realities of the 1960s. Most of the royal party were dressed as though for a wedding, and the Queen was given a hat which recalled medieval modes by Madame Mirman.

By the late 1940s, English men were becoming as tired of drabness and shortages as the women, but in their case the fashion revolt came from below, the young, the working-class lads with money and a craving for style rather than dull subsistence. There had been premonitions from the United States, where in the early 1940s the early zoot-suiters had worn their loose-cut, double-breasted suits with pork-pie hats. In England, shaped up, the suit became the mark of the Spiv, the Flash Harry, the barrow boy or black marketeer. In keeping with the underworld associations such suits were usually worn with trilbies, the flip brim effect shading a rather shifty gaze.

As the world returned to normal, fashion leadership returned to the upper classes. The Edwardian Look was the creation of ex-Guards Officers, their slim-cut Savile Row suits crowned by a curly brimmed bowler, for almost a century their traditional off-duty dress. The downmarket version was the Teddy Boy, but like his zoot-suit predecessors and the Italian-style Mods who succeeded him, he seems to have preferred a soft felt which could be crushed to a pork-pie or a turn-back brim as preferred. The look was Anglo-American, but whatever the form of the headgear it was subordinate to the coiffure.

Elvis Presley and Tony Curtis had projected an image which allowed no place for the hat on the carefully tended quiff or a neatly curled ducktail. Nor were hats popular with their Pop successors, the Beatles: it would have disturbed their well-brushed "bobs."

Hats of a romantic type were taken up by many young men sharing in what the outfitters called the Peacock Revolution. It was inspired by an eclectic historicism; deerstalker hats à la Rex Harrison in *My Fair Lady* mixed with soft shapeless felts and frilly shirts à la Tom Jones given upmarket cachet by Lord Lichfield, the ultimate in society chic, as the Queen's cousin and a successful photographer. Even the conventional young man might find his business felt hat had a Robin Hood pointed brim and feather. The soft romantic thick piled felts went well with the wide-cut suits with deep lapels and broad ties.

But by the late 1960s the Peacock Revolution, flower power, and other youth cults were beginning to founder, as oil prices rose, the slump began, and money for inessentials like fashion was scarce. For those with a social conscience, there were mourning headbands for Vietnam, for those aggressively resistant, the hats of Nazi stormtroopers. As the dreamers returned to reality, and began to hunt for a stake in the world of convention, a job, young men going to the thrift shop, searching for a cast-off trilby to go with their unaccustomed three-piece suit, would often find that the girls, aggressively unisex, had got there before them.

Left: Hats for a royal occasion are illustrated by those worn by the English royal family for the Investiture of the Prince of Wales at Caernarvon Castle in 1968. The Queen's, designed by Simone Mirman, was based on medieval modes. The ladies of the royal family tend to wear variations of the pillbox. It is the matching ensemble which is the feature, rather than the hat itself. The military hats are also a feature.

**Above: Mrs Kennedy set the
style in the mid-1960s, in hats as
well as in so much else. On a
visit to Middleburgh, Virginia,
in February 1962, she wears a**
**pillbox hat with a tweed suit.
As was his usual custom, the
accompanying President was
hatless, a fashion he did much
to promote.**

Conclusion

"No, the 60s and the early 70s were not good years": Freddie Fox, one of the Queen's milliners did not really want to talk about them.

We were talking in his salon, large wood-paneled rooms above London's Bond Street. In one was displayed his designer, or his couture range: in the other the wholesale range. On the far side of the corridor was the workroom. It was almost domestic, the big windows lighting a scene with bright scraps of material, irons, kettles and millinery blocks and heads, some of which (the most cherished) might have smiled blandly on Queen Victoria.

His milliners came from all over the world, bringing traditions from France, Italy and the Orient. There were young and old, those who had worked in the prewar French couture, others who had left well-paid jobs in quite different professions, all because they were obsessed with hats.

At the other end of the trade, I visited the firm of W. Wright, makers of Right Impression, hat-makers of Luton, Bedfordshire, with a hundred years of history. I walked through the back door of their busy modern factory taking the work flow in reverse, past piles of large cardboard boxes, each with the name of its

Left: A couture millinery workroom, that of Philip Somerville in London's West End. The handmade and finished model hats can be adapted to the wearer's color preference, and the basic methods have not changed for centuries. On the table may be seen an example of his fine collection of period hat blocks.

HATS AND ROYAL ASCOT

In June every year at Royal Ascot, a racecourse some ten miles from Windsor — the home of the Sovereign — the wealthy, the nobility and anyone else who wants to go, goes in for a display of headgear — some quite incredible, like the well-known Mrs. Gertrude Shilling, who has always encouraged her milliner designer son David to provide her with something novel each year. It is a tradition that goes back to the days of the Prince Regent, when in 1807 the race called the Ascot Gold Cup was set aside as Ladies' Day.

The course and the "season" were originally established in 1711 by Queen Anne who loved riding and hunting; ignored for some years by the first of the Hanoverians, then revived by the Duke of Cumberland, second son of George II, in 1744, it has continued with few breaks until today. The proximity of Windsor, and the love of someone in the royal family for racing, whether the Prince Regent, William IV, Victoria, or Edward, Prince of Wales — who instituted the Alexandra Plate in 1864 — has meant that there was always a Sovereign's ride from Windsor, and later a parade around the track, an event sure to attract the great,

the good, the gamblers, and the merely curious.

Dressing for Ascot has always been important. Today, with a royal family intensely interested in riding and horse racing, the event is livelier than ever and from the Ascot Office in St. James's Palace each year go forth the regulations regarding dress for those attending the Royal Ascot Enclosure. Menswear remains more formal today than at the time of the Prince Regent, and the gray top hat, once of French silk plush, with a gray band, continues in use with two important changes: the band is black, ever since the "Black Ascot" of 1910 after the death of Edward VII, who as both Prince of Wales and then King, was one of the greatest supporters of the event, and told off even his noble friends if they appeared informally dressed for what, after all, is really a sporting event.

The other change is that French silk plush can no longer be obtained, so that hats now are made from the slightly rougher hair of the hare, according to that most famous of U.K. clothes hiring firms, Moss Bros. And they should know, since they have been hiring out men's clothes for

Ascot for generations.

The ladies, however, have always regarded Ascot as an event for dressing up, and no part of a lady's costume was more important than her hat. In 1827, Queen Adelaide, William IV's wife, was obviously enjoying herself at the races, when it was reported: "The Queen and the Princesses were wearing mantles in the Spanish style with gypsy hats . . .," and this tradition of the royal dress being reported in the newspapers continued. In 1838, the year after her accession, the young Queen Victoria was reported in the *Times* as "wearing a white-drawn gauze bonnet trimmed with pink ribbons and ornamented with artificial roses inside and out . . .," and on Gold Cup Day, the most important day for the ladies: " . . . her bonnet of leghorn straw with ostrich feathers and trimmed with French Sarcenet ribbon having flowers (roses) on the inside . . . "

Sadly, when her consort Prince Albert died and the Queen went into mourning, she forsook Ascot totally, but her son Edward, the Prince of Wales, and his wife Alexandra, continued the tradition to make it even more fashionable as the century wore on.

In her book *Royal Ascot* (1976), Dorothy Laird reminds us of Consuelo, Duchess of Marlborough's, feelings about Ascot around the 1900s:

> I found Ascot week very tiring . . . fortunes were yearly spent on dresses selected as appropriate to a graduated scale of elegance which reached its climax on Thursday; for fashion decreed that one should reserve one's most sumptuous toilette for the Gold Cup Day . . .

Today there is considerable innovation in the women's hats, though the foundation wear of the "Perennial Ascot" can still be seen — that enormous cartwheel made of straw, as Dorothy Laird called it, and which is still regarded as the essential starting point for the upper-class English woman's headgear for fêtes, garden parties, and of course, Ascot.

different chain store destination, the packers, checkers, trimmers, finishers, and the makers with steaming blocks and sewing machines. The storerooms were stacked with brilliant felt and straw hoods from all over the world. Just across the street, I was told, there was a block-making firm, one of the few that remained. It did not take long for an idea to become a saleable hat. And so, through to the showroom, with hats on display from the current factory collection, and on one wall those designed by students from the Royal College of Art whose prestigious postgraduate millinery course is sponsored by the firm.

In the design studio was factory designer Yvette Jelfs. Not much over twenty, pretty, petite and without formal technical training, she learned through systematic determination and an obsessive love of hats.

Bill Horseman, the managing director, is also the Chairman of the Millinery Guild. Over twenty years in the trade, he joined Freddie Fox in a fervent "God Bless the Princess of Wales," the patron saint of modern mainstream millinery and combination ambassadress and trade fair for British fashion. According to Mintel (Market Intelligence) figures, there had been a growth rate of a third between 1984 and 1989, with a rise of 13 percent between 1988 and 1989.

The trade was not doing too badly in the United States either. The Millinery

Right: Royal Ascot 1989, and dressed for the occasion are Princess Diana and the Duchess of York with a friend. Their outfits and those of the racegoers in the background are suitable for the occasion, fashionable yet lighthearted— and it was a sunny day! The hats balance the fashionably broad shoulder line but are not so wide that they dominate the medium short skirt length.

Left: A simple informal cum sports hat for 1989, by Ralph Lauren: traditional, unisex and very much in the Polo style.

Institute had seen a leap in profits: $300 million to $350 million between 1986 and 1987, and foresaw a growth rate of 15 percent. In New York, the link between trade and education was via the Fashion Institute of Technology, where there is close cooperation and a series of Hattitude projects, and publications.

The reason they suggest for the rise in the popularity of hats is a change in fashion initiated in the 1986–87 Paris collections, when a more structured look was introduced, requiring coordinated accessories.

The British Mintel report laid stress on correct dress as a power ploy in the business world. Neither mentioned the ambivalent attitude of the business woman, who often finds women's styles too feminine, and masculine ones too butch. Mintel also notes an increased formality in social life. Weddings might be fewer, but they were also bigger, and there was all that business entertaining

**Above: A hat by Claude
Montana, 1979, illustrates the
fantasy ever present in his
style.**

which boosted the crowds at the fashionable society venues, Ascot and Henley. In England the Thatcher years, in the United States the Reagan years were a time to conform. Even if Yuppies did not wear hats, and statistics showed the 25- to 35-year olds in Great Britain had a low hat-wearing ratio, then their parents certainly did. The older, the more affluent, the more likely you were to wear one.

There is one omission in these reports, no correlation with racial and religious attitudes. A cross-cultural analysis would have been interesting as well as useful, but this was not included.

In Great Britain, the trade prefers to look on the up side; the young get older, and in any case, half of the sample surveyed thought hats a good thing; they kept you warm or shaded; they were definitely on the way back into fashion. As for the 20 percent who thought "hats are not for people like me," well, even they went to weddings, funerals or got colds in the head. They also knew, in the words of young designer Yvette Jelfs, that there were those who were "obsessed with hats" and who appreciated that "People notice people who wear hats . . . they certainly transform the way you look." In any case, business was good. True, interest rates were high, spending power diminishing, but millinery folk wisdom gave you reason to hedge your bets, for a new hat was believed to be the cheapest way to update an old outfit.

The Millinery Information Bureau of America, in spring 1990, had a happy tale

Right: "Dickens," a latter-day top hat in parasisal by Philip Somerville, 1987. The basic shape was introduced into his range in 1984, and the balance of crown and brim has proved infinitely variable.

Opposite page: A dramatic cockade and a curving petal shape of 1984, both made from ribbon, illustrate Kirsten Woodward's inventive sculptural sense.

to tell. The accessory trade was healthy, sales were rising steadily, and they had the medical profession on their side as well as the ecologists, for conservation begins very close to home. If you cover your head, you can cut your personal heat loss by 40 percent. Medical research also suggested that both glaucoma and skin cancer could be reduced by a shady hat. Bobble hats and beach straws from Italy and South East Asia were a large and growing side of the market.

In the meantime the young milliners joyfully explore the possibilities of their métier. Each country has its own galaxy of talent. News of new styles travels fast, for this, as I was told, is "not a trade which can keep a secret"; competition seems an encouragement for the creative.

London is fortunate: it is small enough for a good hat or milliner to stand out. Ascot, Henley, all those royal garden parties give it a unique niche in the fashion year for the summer trade. The recent hot summers have blazed down on a dazzle of subtle shapes, shades and trims. In Europe the trade is a spring and fall one, tying in with the Paris collections, and in the United States there is an emphasis as well on the formalities of the winter season. The globetrotting milliner can have an all-year-round commitment to the smart world.

In her 1983 compilation, *The Fashion Year*, Brenda Polan featured London milliners Alan Couldridge, Freddie Fox, Stephen Jones, David Shilling and Graham Smith. Together with John Boyd, Phillip Sullivan, Kirsten Woodward, they make the current designer millinery market a very exciting scene. All move out from London to accessorize the couture. Brenda Polan saw the hat renaissance as starting with the Vivienne Westwood 1983 collections, a return to the eclectic role dressing of the 1970s, dramatic and with bravura. All the milliners she mentions are still in full and happy creation, making for private clients and a

wholesale trade. Some admit a royal clientele, others do not. After all, like any others, the royal- and fashion-conscious sometimes just like to go out and buy a hat.

All milliners stress the importance of a lady's love affair with her hat. Most of the advanced present-day style trends can be seen in The Hat Shop, run by Carole Denford. Through its prestige outlet in London's Covent Garden, and other branches, it has tried to bring hat style to many young career girls. It stocks models by its own design team and by other young milliners.

Indeed it is the younger members of the trade who make the most definite design statement. Among them, Stephen Jones worked with Vivienne Westwood at the beginning of the London millinery renaissance in 1982–83. He was only just out of college when he put Boy George in a face-framing top hat, an elegantly unisex gesture. The line is one he enjoys working with because of its incisiveness. He is now exploring the asymmetric modes. His hats have appeared at all levels in the media, from international couture shows to pop videos.

It is the artistic possibilities of the hat which attract David Shilling, the milliner perhaps best known to the general public at present. He has made a systematic attempt to promote millinery as an applied art, and has contributed to and organized shows of his hats in museums. He never forgets the lady in the shade of the asymmetric hat brim; after all, the first of his creations to be noticed were the witty creative extravaganzas with which his mother Mrs. Gertrude Shilling delighted the crowds at Ascot. His hats blend romantic charm with inventiveness

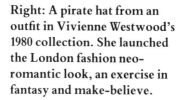

Right: A pirate hat from an outfit in Vivienne Westwood's 1980 collection. She launched the London fashion neo-romantic look, an exercise in fantasy and make-believe.

and a care for color, fit and finish.

Philip Somerville manages to balance graceful innovative hats with the individual needs of his clients and their outfits. His shapes are subtle and he makes interesting use of his magnificent collection of old wooden hats blocks.

There are also those who blend art with craft. The multidimensional sensual appeal of felt has been explored in particular by young hat-makers Victoria Brown and Annie Sherburne, both of whom have worked with Jean Muir. They make their hats by hand-rolling the felt, blending the fibers so as to give it an in-depth variation of color and texture which makes each one unique. In part block made, in part individually molded, there is a subtle link between plastic form and fashionable function. Victoria Brown's Wok hat can be manipulated to suit mood or mode. Annie Sherburne's creations spring from classic traditions, but can have a primitive appeal. A tentative relationship with the Worshipful Company of Feltmakers could have interesting possibilities involving a return to pre-industrial techniques.

In this trade which "cannot keep a secret," it does not take long for an idea to reach the wholesale trade. Bill Horseman of W. Wright had hats in his showroom I remembered from the last season's couture collections. In the twenties and thirties, Wright made the shopping hat, but now that the automobile is in daily use, it is the occasion hat on which they concentrate.

He too remembers the 1960s with a reminiscent shudder, but dates the revival of the hat among young people to Princess Anne's trilby in the 1970s. He

Left: Stephen Jones distils new fantasies from "Flamenco", a close-fitting cocktail hat of foliate-edged felt with a turquoise crown; from his Tales of the Alhambra collection, autumn–winter 1986–87.

Right: A harmonious counterpoint of multilayered straw by David Shilling, 1986, illustrates his dynamic use of form. Called "Hat Trick", the top layer can be lifted off to be lent to a friend!

Opposite page: The Wok hat of 1988 by Victoria Brown can be worn in many different ways, and the handmade felt has great variety and depth of tone.

remembers producing upmarket Baker Boy berets for the general trade. They were very useful cold-weather wear, foam-lined and with a scarf through the loop. Another successful adaptation was the romantic Biba hat, with the strategically placed holes, in the felt. But, it was with the Disco hat that Wright's bounced to the top: inspired by John Travolta's *Saturday Night Fever* (1977), they made 60,000, cornering the market on price because they made them from molded plastic, cheaper than sewing them.

Since then the firm has produced many versions of Princess Diana's hats. The average young Englishwoman is happy to follow her lead. Indeed John Boyd hats of the early 1980s, tilted toques with a curving flourish of feathers, spent seven years in their line: a classic of late 20th-century fashion!

But the largest producer of European women's headwear is Kangol, whose design director is couture milliner Graham Smith. The name of the firm combines angora and wool, with an added K, the materials of the beret on which the firm's fortunes were founded. It was started by Jacques Spreiregen, a Polish-born Frenchman, who moved to England in the late 1930s. They profited from the vogue for sporty Basque berets in the late 1930s, and when the war came, the demand from the army. As General Montgomery showed, the beret jaunty and resilient had advantages over the traditional type of army cap. The present managing director, George Dan, is now developing the fashion side to which Graham Smith is making his contribution by retaining the classic appeal but giving it a new fashionable dimension.

The Mintel report finds men more reluctant hat-wearers than women, except where extra warmth is needed. For the modern hatter, with access to current medical opinion, their patron saint St. Clement's tonsure, his bald patch, has as much significance as the wool scrunched between his toes for the early felt-maker.

Christy and Sons of Stockport, now an amalgamation of five firms in the men's hat trade, can, with the accumulated expertise of over two hundred years,

cope wherever male hat preference lies. Their production is divided into felt and wool hats and caps, and they have an emphasis on sports and riding wear. A high proportion of their product is exported especially to the United States, Japan, France, Italy and Germany. Their design team organizes their range so that there is something for everyone and agents feed back local style preferences. The differences are subtle: a dramatic change in the balance of the fashionable suit, from broad to narrow shoulders can mean a change of just an inch in a hat brim. With long historical perspective, they see the traffic-free pedestrian zones as an additional boost for their sales.

Which way will it go, the hat and millinery trade at the end of the 20th century? It makes a design statement acceptable even in applied art terms, and puts the finishing touch to a smart outfit. But an important aspect of its appeal, or lack of it, goes to the roots of the personality. To Janet Sloane, hat publicist with long experience: "Its appeal is emotional, based on impulse, based on someone's likes and dislikes, not necessarily absolute." Beyond this area of indecision, of perennial optimism triumphing over experience, is a long career protecting, identifying and providing in 19th-century hatter Henry Mellows' words "Hats for the Heads of the People." In a world of changing climates, frontiers and role models, there will be much for it to do.

Right: Princess Diana in the tip-tilted toque with swooping flourish of feathers, the type of hat which she wore in the early 1980s. This was designed by John Boyd in 1982. It was a style which became universally popular.

Left: A summer hat by Graham Smith, 1989, recalls the wide trimmed Edwardian fantasies in a contemporary way.

Above: Hat styles as promoted by the Millinery Institute of New York in 1990: a white straw in the style of the 1930s and a red felt toque, both by Frank Olive; a cocktail cap by Don Anderson.

Right: Abstract sculptural flyaway shape in stiffened guipure by Philip Treacy, final-year student at the Royal College of Art, London.

Right: The Hat Conformator was invented in the mid-19th century by M. Maillard to simplify hat fitting by measuring the head in all its dimensions.

Glossary

The modern milliner and hatter often uses historical or trade terms to describe the styles they create, and this glossary may help to elucidate. It will also provide a brief overall view of hats around the world.

Almuce A hood usually lined with fur.

Alpine or Tyrolese hat Hat with a conical crown and narrow straight brim, often trimmed with cord hatband and feather and based on the peasant hat of that area.

Amice A white ritual hood worn by priests.

Anthony Eden hat see **Homburg**.

Ascot A gray top hat invented by London hat firm of J. Locke for wear at Ascot races.

Babushka A colloquial term for a Russian woman's head scarf, deriving from the word for grandmother, traditionally those who wear it.

Bachlik A short cape with a hood from the Balkans.

Baku A straw with a dull finish made from the young stalks of the Talipot palm from Malabar and Ceylon.

Balaclava (helmet) A knited hood which covers head, ears and neck and can be drawn up to shield the mouth. Much used by soldiers and travelers, its name derives from the Battle of Balaclava, in the Crimean War, 1854, but it existed in 1843, as The Protector, patented by James Martin of Walworth.

Balibuntal Straw fiber woven in Luzon in the Philippines, and in Thailand, also Bintal.

Balmoral A beret-like cap associated with Scottish folk dress, taking its name from Queen Victoria's Highland home. Also called the **Kilmarnock**.

Bambini A hat with a halo brim taking its name from the rounded plaques of the Bambino designed by Della Robbia in Florence.

Bandeau A stiffened band to lift the hat from the head, also a half hat.

Bangkok Fine light palm fiber grown and woven near Bangkok.

Barbe Also barbette, georgette, and wimple, covered the ladies' head, neck and sometimes chin. At its most concealing used for mourning in 15th and 16th centuries.

Barrentino Small Italian cap used by fishermen and farmers.

Batt The felt shape during its processing into a hat.

Bavolet A frill at the back of the 19th-century bonnet which may have taken its name from the voluminous peasant coifs worn in France.

Beanie Modern U.S. term for skullcap.

Beaver An aquatic mammal, the *castor* whose underfur makes the highest quality hat felt. See **Castor**.

Beefeater A black beret-shaped felt hat with small brim and cockade in 16th-century style, or gathered soft felt hat, traditionally worn by the Yeomen of the Guard and Warders of the Tower of London.

Beguin, Biggon, biggin A close-fitting cap usually made in three pieces and worn by both men and women in medieval times. Worn by a 12th-century order of lay sisters from which it took its name. In 18th century had wide sidepieces.

Beret Round flat cap worn by Basque peasantry having a central string called a tontarra. Very popular for sportswear with both sexes.

Beret, Scotch Soft round cap derived from traditional wear in Scotland. Also **Glengarry, Kilmarnock, Tam-O'-Shanter**.

Bersagliere Hat or plume. Based on that of the Italian mountain regiment, it is worn at an angle, has a wide brim and large curving feather mount.

Bibi A bonnet worn in the 1830s. The term is of uncertain origin and may reflect its nonsense or babyish quality.

Bicorne A hat with the turned-up brim forming two points, a 19th-century term for a survival of 18th-century style now used for ceremonial, court, military, and naval dress.

Billycock A bowler hat, c.1850, popularly named after William Coke. Also a casual hat worn by late 18th-century gangs of "Bullies".

Bird of paradise Species of beautifully plumed birds from South East Asia and North Australia used in 19th and early 20th centuries for hat decoration, but now protected.

Biretta A square cap with raised seams worn catty-corner on the head. Of medieval origin it is in current ecclesiastical use by Cardinals in red, bishops in purple and priests in black. It is also worn in full dress by some senior academics. See also **Trencher cap**.

Block Mold on which hat is shaped. Originally wood but now metal as part of the factory process.

Blocker Slang term for **Bowler**.

Boater Hat made from braided straw, waterproofed with shellac, and having a straight crown and a narrow straight brim. Originally a sailor's hat, it was adopted for general and sports wear by both men and women from the end of the 19th century. It is also, especially in the U.S., known as a **Sennit**, from the seven-unit braid method, and in France as a **Canotier**.

Bolero Hat based on Spanish folk hats with flat crowns and straight medium brims.

Bollinger A mid-19th-century informal man's hat with a low round crown and a flat brim.

Bonnet Ladies' headdress covering the back of the head and having the brim in funnel form to shade the face. See also **Calache**.

Borsalino Man's fur felt hat from name of the Italian firm which made it, particularly popular in the 1920s, and of exceptionally fine quality and workmanship.

Boudoir or Curler cap A decorative cap worn by a lady in her bedroom to cover undressed hair curlers. Very popular in the 1920s when they were also known as Shingle caps.

Bourlet Face opening of the hood in the 15th century, often padded as the foundation of the chaperon.

Bowler A stiff felt hat with a low round crown and a narrow brim. The prototype was made for the London firm of Locke & Co. by the feltmakers Bowler for a client William Coke in the 1840s, hence the names by which it is known. See also **Billycock, Blocker, Christie, Derby**.

Breton sailor hat A hat with low crown and wide upturned brim, deriving from type of man's traditional Breton hat.

Brim The bottom border of the hat.

Bucket hat Modern U.S. term for a sports hat with round dented crown made from waterproof material.

Buriti Fiber from Brazilian palm used for making straw hats.

Busby A tall fur hat now best known as the 'Bearskin', worn for parade dress by the Brigade of Guards in the U.K. It consists of fur mounted over a wicker foundation.

Butterfly headdress Veil supported on wires to give the effect of wings, fashionable in the late 15th century.

Bycocket A 15th-century term with variable definitions but usually thought to describe a man's hat with brim turrned up front and back and pulled into a peak at the side.

Cabriolet bonnet 18th-century bonnet shaped like the hood of a light carriage of that name.

Calache or Calash A protective folding hood worn to protect high headdress c.1770s-1830s and made like a sunbonnet.

Calpack (Shapka) Traditional Cossack fur cap, cylindrical and often of curly lamb's wool.

Canotier see **Boater**.

Cap A generic term for a head covering, usually in soft material and worn by both men and women. Currently for men, it generally has a peak and is classified according to the number of panels in the crown. Thus one-piece, five-piece, etc.

Capeline A felt hood blocked with preliminary shaping into that of a hat with a brim. Also used for a felt hat with a brim.

Capotain or Copotain A high conical cap fashionable in the 16th century.

Capote A 19th-century French term for a fashionable bonnet.

Capuchin, Capuchon A hood with a shoulder cape.

Cardinal An 18th-century ladies' hooded cloak.

Cardinal's hat Deriving from the medieval traveling hat, it has a low crown, a flat brim and is hung from the cords with a ritual number of tassels.

Carroting In feltmaking, the treatment of the hair with mercury and nitric acid which improved its bonding quality. The term came from the color that the compound gave to the hair tips.

Cartwheel A modern term for a ladies' hat with a wide round, shallow crown.

Castor Beaver (Fr.) and the colloquial French and English term for a hat made from its felted fur. Despite guild quality regulations it soon became a generic term for any kind of fur felt, whatever its fiber content. By the 19th century it was also used for the **Top hat**, which was originally made with silk on a felt base.

Caudebec A town in Normandy which in the 18th century gave its name to a cheap form of felt hat also known as a **Cordy**.

Caul A decorative hairnet for women and also worn by men in the 16th century.

Chapeau Bras (Fr.), **Carried hat** (Eng.) A hat required by etiquette, shaped for portability not wear. Introduced in the later 18th century, it continues in ceremonial use. See **Bicorne**.

Chaperon A hood (Fr.), but usually applied to the turban twisted form fashionable in the 15th century.

Chaplet 15th-century, a padded roll for a headdress.

Chechia A Zouave cap, cylindrical and brimless.

Chimney A term for a late-15th-century ladies' tall headdress.

Chimney Pot A man's tall top hat.

Chip Slivers of wood, usually willow and larch, interwoven to make hats or bonnets.

Christie The Canadian term for **Bowler** or **Derby**, deriving from the London firm of J. Christie and Co. from whom many were imported.

Cloche A tightfitting hat pulled low over the forehead, characteristic of fashion hats in the 1920s.

Cloud See also **Fascinator**, a loosely made light scarf worn over the head and shoulders in the late 19th century.

Clown hat A high pointed cap worn by some clowns in circuses and derived from dress worn in Italian Commædia Dell'Arte.

Coal-heaver hat With protective flap-cum-brim at the back. An 18th-century trade hat, it has inspired 20th-century fashionable shapes.

Coal scuttle Slang term for the 19th-century bonnet with large brim.

Cockade A ribbon bow deriving from the tie attaching the brim of a cocked hat. Originally decorative, it was also used as political identification; thus the white cockade was worn by the Jacobites, and the Tricoleur by the French Republicans.

Cocked hat A hat which is styled with the brim turned up, particularly applied to styles of the 17th and 18th century.

Coif Medieval to 17th-century term for a close-fitting head covering, worn by men but in the later period mainly by women.

Coiffure Any method of dressing the head or hair.

Commander The string used to force down the felt hood on the block in the hand felt hat-making process in the 18th century.

Commode A wire frame on which the late-17th-century high ladies' headdress was adjusted.

Conformateur Invented by M. Maillard in the 19th-century to map out the three-dimensional shape of the head and make customer fitting easier.

Coolie or Chinese hat Made in one piece, wide and rising to a peak in the centre. Usually of straw.

Coguard A Swiss or German 16th-century-type man's hat copiously edged with feather.

Cordy see **Cavdebec**.

Cornet Late-17th and 18th-century ladies' cap with pendant sidepieces.

Cottage bonnet Usually straw with straight brim and worn in early 19th century.

Couvrechef A veil or covering for the head.

Cowboy hat, Western hat, Ten-gallon hat, Stetson A felt hat with low dented crown and wide brim adapted for the cattle herders of the American West and owing some of its shape to the Mexican sombrero.

Cowl An ecclesastical hood, especially the loose hood worn by monks.

Crepin, Crespin A cap with metal thread and openwork trim.

Crinoline hat Made from Crin or horsehair and vegetable fiber of the

fibers of the palm, *Crin Vegetale*.

Crush hat or opera hat Collapsible silk top hat, see also **Gibus**.

Crusher hat Soft felt hat flexible enough to be rolled in a pocket.

Davy Crockett hat Fat cap with pendant animal tail, named after U.S. politician, Indian scout and mighty hunter, 1786-1836.

Deerstalker A hunting and traveling cap originating in the mid-19th century and having front and back peaks, earflaps and a crown, reversing to scarlet. It is often associated with the fictional detective Sherlock Holmes. A version was called the Fore and Aft.

Demicastor 17th- and 18th-century term for hat with surface finished with beaver hair.

Derby hat The American term for the **Bowler** because of its popularity at the Derby horse race, when worn by the Earl of Derby.

Doll's hat Very small ladies' hats fashionable in the 1930s and early 1940s.

Doré (Fr.), **plated** (Eng.) Term applied to the technique of making the outer surface of a felt hat superior to the inside by using better-quality materials.

Dormeuse A late-18th-century woman's cap; from French for "sleeper", it was enveloping and comparatively simple, an informal style.

Easter bonnet A new hat purchased for wear on Easter Sunday, a traditional time for a new spring outfit.

Egret White plume from various heron species prized as hat trimming but no longer permitted to be used. It is also applied to other feathers made up to look similar.

Escoffion A late medieval headdress, based on a jeweled caul which was stuffed into various shapes such as horns.

Estridge felt 16th-century felt imported from Europe. It is often confused with ostrich felt, itself a misprint: in an 18th-century text Laine D'Autriche (Austrian wool) became Laine D'Autruche (ostrich wool).

Eugenie hat A tip-tilted ladies' hat with low crown and small curled brim, popular in the 1930s and so-called because of its alleged resemblance to hats worn by the Empress Eugenie in the 1860s.

Fanchon Fr. for "kerchief", a bonnet of the 1860s, small, triangular and made with brim and crown in one.

Fascinator see **Cloud**.

Feathers Popular trimming for hats. There are now strict controls on the use of many species, and after 1941 an agreement was reached with the plumage trade in U.S. that no wild bird feathers should be used.

Fedora A man's felt hat with low crown, centre crease and rolled brim for informal wear. Introduced in 1881 inspired by Sardou's play *Fedora*.

Felt A basic material for hats since early times, its characteristic is that the fibers are compressed and molded into fabric, not spun and woven. Now generally divided into wool felt and fur felt. Many kinds of fiber are used, natural and synthetic.

Fez A man's cone-shaped cap with a flat top, without a brim, usually red and trimmed with a tassel, which was prescribed wear for Turks and people in the Turkish Empire from the early 19th century. In 1923 in Republican Turkey under Kemal Ataturk it became illegal, though it was still worn in countries in the former Turkish sphere of influence. Named from the town of Fez, in Morocco. See also **Tarboosh**.

Flat cap 16-century cap usually knitted with flat top and of beret-like form. Was and sometimes is usual wear of London tradesmen. See **Statute cap**.

Fontange A bow on a ladies' headdress worn in the late 17th and early 18th centuries, named after The Duchesse de Fontanges. The term is often incorrectly applied to the whole headdress.

Forehead cloth or Cross cloth 16th- and 17th-century term for a band covering the front of a woman's head. It was often triangular.

Forage cap Originally a soft high cap with a peak adopted by the U.S. cavalry as "undress" during the American Civil War; deriving from the cap worn by French troops in Algeria, the **Kepi**, which in turn was borrowed from the German army.

Four and niner Slang for a hat based on the London selling prices (four shillings and nine pence). Mid 19th-century.

Fret A medieval hairnet.

French hood 16th-century, rounded and worn off a lady's face.

Frontlet A decorative covering for the front of a woman's hood in the 15th and 16th centuries.

Gable or Pediment 16th-century ladies' headdress supported into a shape like the pointed side of a roof.

Gainsborough Hat inspired by late-18th-century portraits, especially by that painter, illustrating hats with large soft brims and feather trimming.

Gandhi cap A traditional Indian cap, boat-shaped and associated with Mahatma Gandhi, the Indian political leader, who wore Indian traditional dress.

Garibaldi Pillbox hat as worn by Italian Independence leader and popular hero Giuseppe Garibaldi in the 1850s.

Gaucho hat As worn by South American cattle herders, and characterized by its Spanish-style flat crown as well as its broad brim.

Gibus A folding top hat invented by the Paris hatter Antoine Gibus. Patents for it were issued to him between 1834 and 1840.

Glengarry cap Worn with Scottish military and traditional dress but introduced in 1805 for Clan Glengarry. It is oval with a central crease and is trimmed with a tartan ribbon around the head opening, streamers and a clan badge.

Gob cap Name given to the cap of the enlisted man in the U.S. navy from 1940. It is white cotton with a four-piece crown and a full stitched brim. (Gob is derived from Canadian-Scottish "gobbie", meaning fisherman.)

Gondolier hat As worn by Venetian boatmen, it has wide brim and shallow crown. Sometimes worn with a decorative hairnet.

Gorget or Gole Medieval, the shoulder opening of the hood.

Gorro Catalan stocking cap.

Gossamer or Gossie A top hat with treated muslin foundation introduced in about 1834. In the U.S., the term was used in 1888 for a light waterproof hat.

Hatband A trimming for the hat usually arranged at the junction of brim and crown, and an important decorative feature.

Havelock A white cloth covering attached to a cap to protect the back of the neck, introduced by General Sir Henry Havelock for soldiers during the Indian mutiny in 1857. It is a feature of some sports caps.

Head rail A medieval veil, covering the head.

Helmet Hard hat based on soldier's helmet of 19th century, having peak and pointed oval profile.

Henin A medieval term now used for various forms of high headdress fashionable in the 15th century.

Homburg or Anthony Eden A hard felt hat with slightly tapering Tyrolean-inspired crown shaped with a central crease and having a brim, ribbon-bound, with a slight curl at the side. It was popularized by Edward VII who introduced it when staying in Homburg, the German spa.

Hood A basic covering for the head worn at all times in all countries and by both sexes in many styles and sometimes attached to a cloak. It is usually made of woven fabric and is mainly utilitarian in function. The term is also used for a hat before its final shaping.

Horned headdress The 15th-century ladies' headdress with curved sidepoints.

Horsehair A semi-rigid fabric made from horsehair or synthetics with the same appearance and much used in hatmaking. One substitute is the palm, *Crin Vegetale*. See also **Crinoline**.

Houve A medieval cap or hood.

Huke Folk, 16th- and 17th-century; an enveloping combination cloak, hood, and veil.

Hunting cap Functional and protective, varying according to the sport. For riding it is reinforced and has a peak; for shooting it is sometimes made in red or with red trim.

Hure, Huer A medieval cap, probably felted.

Jester cap A hood with bell-trimmed peaks deriving from that worn by the medieval jester. Often called Cap and Bells.

Jinnah cap The traditional cap of Pakistan, a karakul tarboosh, and named for Mohammed Ali Jinnah, founder of Pakistan, and first Governor General.

Juliet cap A skull cap worn by women and usually prettily trimmed, so-called by costume worn for Shakespeare's *Romeo and Juliet*.

Jockey cap or Jockei (Fr.) A peaked cap, originally worn for hunting

in the 18th century but adopted into female fashion during the Directoire.

Keffiyah Arab headdress consisting of a cloth placed protectively on the head and held with the Agal, a binding cord.

Kennel headdress see **Gable**.

Kepi (Fr.) Military hat of mid 19th-century with peak, slanting front and straight back.

Khevenhuller A popular man's hat early- to mid-18th-century, named after Austrian Fieldmarshal Ludwig Andreas Khevenhuller, 1683-1744, and distinguished by the deep front turnup of the brim, with small pinch, peaks at the sides, and a small turnup at the back.

Kilmarnock see **Beret**.

Korean hat Traditional for men, a tall black hat with medium-wide brim tied under the chin.

Kulah A conical hat worn in the Middle East, especially by priests and dervishes.

Lancer's feather Trimming modeled on Lancer's plume.

Lappet 18th- and 19th-century, pendant trimmings, usually of lace, from ladies' cap.

Leghorn Fine straw hats which owed their quality to the type of wheat grown in Tuscany, and to the traditional skill in their making.

Liberty & Co. London store with reputation from late 19th century for advanced design in hats. "Liberty-style" is the European term for Aesthetic styles in the late 19th century.

Liberty cap see **Phrygian cap**.

Ligne (Fr.) Measuring unit of 1/11th inch, used for ribbon and binding.

Liripipe or Tippet Medieval pendant trimming, sometimes from a hood.

Macaroni hat Small three-cornered hat as worn by Macaronis, groups of over-smart young men-about-town, c.1770s.

Mackinaw U.S. man's hat of coarse straw with flexible brim.

Mahrharmah Turkish woman's hood which also covers the face, worn out of doors.

Mandarin hat Popularly a black silk hat with deep turnup brim, and pointed crown with button at top, as worn by Chinese nobles of Manchu dynasty.

Marabou feathers Soft and downy from the adjutant crane.

Marquise hat A modern version of the 18th-century ladies' cocked hat.

Melusine Silk fabric with pile finish popular for hats.

Merry Widow hat Popular about 1907 and similar to the **Gainsborough hat** with big brim and feather trim. Took its name from the musical of that name, produced in London.

Milan straw Straw braid and hats from Milan, Italy.

Milliner, Millinery Since the 19th century, the trade and popular term for one who makes trims, and sells hats. See also **Modiste**.

Mitre An oval ceremonial cap worn by a bishop.

Mob cap A soft, washable ladies' cap introduced in the late 18th century and now almost generic for any costumiers' period-style cap.

Modiste (Fr.) see **Milliner**.

Monk's hood see **Cowl**.

Monmouth cap Knitted woolen cap, usually conical, popular with sailors and soldiers in the 16th and 17th centuries and having a weather-resistant felted finish. Their manufacture was the specialty of the Welsh border town of Monmouth.

Montego hat Coconut palm hats from Montego Bay, Jamaica.

Montero or Eugenie Wig A hunting and traveling cap of Spanish origin popular from the 17th century, with earflaps and a turnedup brim. Empress Eugenie presented some to the French Arctic exhibition in 1864, hence the 19th-century slang term.

Mortar board see **Trencher cap**.

Muffin cap Similar in shape to a flat bun and popular cold weather wear for children in the 19th century.

Muller Cut Down A flat-crowned bowler popular in the 1860s and so-called after a murderer, Muller, who had worn one.

Mushroom hat With oval crown and down-curved wide brim.

Negligée cap 18th-century term for a cap worn within the house and informally.

Nightcap Worn in bed or in the 16th to 18th centuries informally within the house. Those worn by men in the 18th century are often fine and decorative. (Colloquially a comfort drink before sleeping.)

Nithsdale A traveling cloak with a hood, so-called after Lady Nithsdale disguised her husband, a Jacobite, in one, during his escape from the Tower of London in 1716.

Nivernois Small cocked hat fashionable c.1765-1780 and called after the French Ambassador to England 1762-3, Louis-Jules Mancini Mazarini, Duke of Nevenois 1716-1798.

Opera hat see **Crush hat**.

Osprey Very popular feather trimmings in the 19th and 20th centuries before the advent of Bird preservation measures. They were fine, with a delicate curve, and usually white. They come from the egret, or "fishing hawk" as it was known.

Ostrich feathers Popular feather trimmings since early times. The birds were farmed in South Africa from 1865, but they are now a protected species.

Panache A tuft of feathers used as trimming.

Panama hat Woven from straw of the jipijapa (toquilla) plant growing in Ecuador, Colombia and Peru. It was first sold in Panama, hence the term. Very light, fine and flexible, they are of high quality and expensive.

Pedal straw The lower part of a cornstalk, also pedal straw braid

Pedaline. The hat made from pedal straw, or similar synthetic imitations.

Pellon U.S. brand name of a mixture of bonded man-made and natural fibers with moldable and shape-retention qualities often used for hats. Made by the Pellon Corporation.

Petasos A wide-brimmed traveling hat worn in classical Greece.

Phrygian cap As worn by the inhabitants of ancient Phrygia in the Peloponnese, it became the archetypal cap of classical Greece and Rome where it was the mark of a free citizen. It was soft and bag-shaped. During the French Revolution it was adopted as the Cap of Liberty and was usually red.

Picture hat In romantic mode with wide brim and much trimming, usually worn for semiformal occasions such as weddings, garden parties, etc.

Pilgrim hat A medieval traveling hat usually having a wide brim and souvenir badges from the shrines visited, such as cockleshells. See also **Sugar Loaf**.

Pillbox Small flat round hat without a brim, also called a Page, Bellboy's or Busboy's cap from its use in hotel uniforms.

Pilos, Pileus Close-fitting headgear worn in ancient Greece and Rome.

Pinch front The front of the crown of a hat when shaped by indentations at the side.

Pinner A simple 17th- and 18th-century cap pinned into place.

Pith Helmet or Topee Used by Europeans in the tropics as protection against the sun. Usually helmet-shaped, insulated with pith from the Indian spongewood plant, and cloth covered. The Topee is insulated with cork.

Planter's hat Made from straw, with wide brim.

Plated see **Doré**

Poke bonnet Fashionable from the late-18th to the mid-19th-century and usually comprizing a wide brim enclosing the sides of the head. There are many possible sources for the term – the projection of the brim or the shape of the crown or poke.

Pork-pie hat Fashionable for women dining 1855-65 with flat crown and upturned brim. A man's informal hat fashion especially in the 1930s and 1940s, so-called because the crease all round the inside of the crown made it resemble a pork pie.

Postillion hat With tapering flat-topped crown and narrow straight brim inspired by the dress of 18th-century outriders, but used by ladies and gentlemen from the late 18th century to the early 19th century.

Puggaree, Pugree, Pagri Turban as worn in India, an informally draped length of fabric.

Puritan hat see **Sugar Loaf**.

Quaker hat Bonnet of various types as prescribed by the Society of Friends for their members and usually plain, avoiding current fashion. In the 1770s, the term was used in France for a man's round hat, as worn by Benjamin Franklin.

Ramie A plant from East Asia used as a source for hat fiber.

Ramillies cock Early-18th-century man's hat named after battle of Ramillies, 1706, and having the back turned up higher than the front.

Robin Hood hat Popular in 1960s, having a conical crown and narrow brim turned tightly up at the back.

Roughrider Type of cowboy hat worn by U.S. Cavalry Volunteers led by Theodore Roosevelt in the Spanish-American War, 1898.

Sailor hat Differs according to the navy but currently generally with flat shape. Historically and internationally, sailor hats have taken many forms: of straw, flat with wide brims and low crowns made from waterproofed fabric in the 19th century; with a pompom on the crown, French, and with streamers at the back, German. See also **Boater** and **Gob**.

Sennit see **Boater**.

Shadow 16th and early-17th-century woman's hood wired and extended above head level. A variant of the Bongrace, it was used for protection against the sun.

Shako A military cap as worn by the Hungarians in the early 19th century, having a peak and crown-like truncated cone and trimmed with a plume.

Shape The frame used for a hat or bonnet.

Shovel hat As worn by Roman Catholic priests in outdoor dress. It has a low round crown and a turnup on the brim sides which makes the front and back project like a shovel.

Silk hat see **Top hat**.

Ski cap Worn for the sport, it has earflaps and a brim.

Skimmer see **Boater**.

Skullcap A round cap covering only the top of the head. See also **Yarmulke**.

Slouch hat Having a broad and drooping brim.

Smoking cap Mid-19th-century decorative informal cap, usually pillbox shape, supposed to be worn by gentlemen when smoking, to protect from the smell.

Snap brim Soft felt hat with brim turned down sharply in front, popularized by the Prince of Wales in 1922.

Snood Band for holding hair in place and, in 19th-century Scotland, worn by young unmarried women. Also a decorative openwork bag to cover the hair at the back. See also **Caul**.

Sombrero Spanish and South American hat, thus called because it shades from the sun. It has a high dented crown and a wide deeply rolling brim.

Sou'wester A protective hat against rain, so-called because it is worn at sea in stormy weather. Made from waterproofed material, it generally has a brim broadening at the back, earflaps and a chin tie.

Sparterie A basic material in hat making, which can be used to stiffen and to make the shape. Moldable when damp, it consists of muslin-faced mixture of plant and horsehair fibers.

Spoon bonnet Fashionable in the 1860s and so-called because it resembled in shape the bowl of a spoon.

Statute cap Prescribed by an Act of Parliament in 1571-93 to be made from English wool and worn on Sundays and holidays by those not of the nobility. See also **Flat cap**.

Steeple crown hat Having a high pointed crown and flat brim, and fashionable in the early 17th century.

Stetson Strictly a hat made by the U.S. firm J.B. Stetson Co., who made fine-quality felt hats, but often transferred to their most popular line, the cowboy hat.

Stocking cap A long cylindrical cap usually knitted in the round, hence the term.

Stovepipe see **Top hat**.

Straw Plait Made from braided straws which are stitched together into hat form. There were important centers of manufacture in the English East Midlands, Switzerland, Germany, Austria and Italy. See **Leghorn, Milan,** and **Straw**.

Sugar Loaf hat 16th-to early-17th-century, having a crown shaped like a conical loaf of sugar.

Sunbonnet Summer headgear for country women in the 19th and 20th centuries with frills to shade the eyes and protect the neck. made from fabric gathered over stiffening wires or slats, hence the alternative term Slatbonnet.

Tarboosh Close-fitting cap of cloth or felt, usually red, with a flat top and with a tassel usually of blue silk, worn by Muslims in the Arabic world. See also **Fez** — the Turkish version.

Tagal Plaited manila hemp from Tagal in Java, used to make lightweight hats.

Tam-O'-Shanter, Tam, Tammy Soft woollen cap with flat floppy circular crown derived from the cap or bonnet worn by Scottish ploughmen in the 18th century and called after Robert Burns's poem of that name in 1786. In the 1880s it became very popular for women and young girls.

Telescope hat U.S., a hat with a circular fold around the inside of the crown and straight sides.

Templers, Templettes 15th-century; extension of the coronet to cover the peaks of hair at the temples.

Ten-gallon hat see **Cowboy hat**.

Thanet Bowler with low crown made by Locke's of London to the order of the Earl of Thanet in the mid 19th century.

Tholia Feminine straw hat of Ancient Greece, wide and flat with a peaked crown.

Thrummed caps Mainly 18th-century, soft wool caps with a weather-resistant piled finish.

Tiara Headdress, usually of jewels.

Titfa or titva Cockney rhyming slang: "Tit for Tat" = "Hat".

Tobaggan cap Worn for the sport. A patterned stocking cap usually trimmed with a pompom.

Top hat, topper Also chimney pot, beaver, bell topper, golgotha (Oxford University slang), silk hat, Stovepipe. A stiff high hat with rolled brim made on a rigid foundation. Introduced at the end of the 18th century, very popular in the mid-19th century and now worn for only the most formal occasions, though a variant is used as a formal riding hat. It is usually made from black silk, though gray felt can be worn for formal day wear.

Topee see **Pith Helmet**.

Toque From Italian Tocca, a cap, and in use by 1505. Usually used for a hat without a brim.

Toreador hat Inspired by the close-fitting black hat with turnedup brim, wider at the sides, of the Spanish Toreador.

Tower High headdresss fashionable in the late 17th and early 18th centuries.

Toyo hat Lightweight hat made of paper braid that looks like straw.

Tremont hat U.S. felt hat with tapered crown and narrow brim, c.1950s.

Trencher cap, Mortar board or Cater cap Formal wear for some (especially English) academics. Deriving from 15th-century styles it consists of a skullcap to which is affixed a flat square crown with tassel; hence the name, from the old type of plate or trencher, or the board for mixing cement. It is worn with a point to the front. See also **Biretta.**

Tricorne From French late-18th-century term for hat with turnedup brim and having three corners.

Trilby Soft felt hat with rolled brim which became fashionable at the time of Du Maurier's novel *Trilby* in the 1890s, and which has remained fashionable ever since.

Turban Eastern and Near Eastern headdress made from length of fabric draped into cushion-like shape. Fashionable ladies' hat made in the same style.

Tyrolean hat With sharply tapered crown and narrow brim, with cord band and feather mount, usually in green rough-textured fabric and based on the folk hats of the Tyrol.

Veil Semi-transparent drape decoratively concealing the features in a fashionable hat. Also in some places and religions considered essential concealment of a woman's face in public, e.g., that worn by Muslim women, the yashmak.

Watch cap A knitted cap, usually dark blue with turnedup borders, which originated in the U.S. navy for wear on watch in cold weather.

Weepers Heavy hatband of black crepe worn by male mourners at a funeral, in the 19th and early 20th centuries.

Western hat see **Cowboy hat**.

Wideawake A soft felt hat c.1840, with large brim and low crown, allegedly so-called because (*Punch*, 1844), "It never has a nap, and never needs one".

Widow's cap Has assumed many styles over the centuries (see **Barbe**), but since the 16th century has been characterized by a close fit and a point over the forehead, and these general features were still present in the 19th century, and adopted, for example, by Queen Victoria in her widowhood.

Wimple A medieval covering for the head, usually of linen, that extends down and covers the neck. See also **Barbe**.

Witch's hat A pointed black hat with a narrow brim deriving from early-17th-century-style hats and associated with fanciful illustrations based on 17th-century woodcuts of witch trials showing old ladies of the period.

Yachting cap Loosely based on naval uniform and made with flat top and peak in navy blue and white, usually with a badge on the front.

Yarmulke A skullcap ritually worn by Jewish men.

Zuchetto A small skullcap worn by Italian priests to cover the tonsure. See also **Biretta.**

Bibliography

Almanac des negociants (1762)
Arnold, J., *Queen Elizabeth's Wardrobe Unlock'd* (1988)
Art of Dress (1830)
Arts and Crafts of Ribbon Work (1924)
Baker, L., *Hatpins and Hatpin Holders* (1982)
Baldwin, F. E., *Sumptuary Legislation in England* (1926)
Ballin, A. J., *Science of Dress* (1877)
Baumgarten, L., *Eighteenth Century Clothes Taken From Colonial Williamsburg* (1986)
Bloomingdale's Catalogue 1887 (Facsimile edition)
Book of Trades (1804-5, 1818, 1835)
Brand, V., *Millinery* (1935)
Briggs, A., *Victorian Things* (1986)
Booth, C., *Life and Labour of the People of London, Vol V11* (1896)
Buck, A. M., *Victorian Costume and Accessories* (1954/61); *Dress in Eighteenth Century England* (1979)
Buckland, K., *The Monmouth Cap* (Costume 13, 1979)
Burkett, M., *The Art of the Feltmaker* (1979)
Byrde, P. A., *Frivolous Distinction: fashion and needlework in the works of Jane Austen* (1979); *The Male Image: men's fashion in England 1300-1970* (1979)
A Cavalry Officer, *The Whole Art of Dress* (1830)
Campbell, R., *The London Tradesman* (1748)
Celnart, Mme., *Manuel des Dames* (1829)
Chambers Journal, pp327-328 (1855)
Cherichetti, D., *Hollywood Costume Design* (1876)
CIBA Review, *Hats* (no. 40); *Felt* (no. 149)
Clabburn, P. *A Provincial Milliners Shop in 1785* (Costume 11, 1975)
Clark, F., *Hats* (1983)
Cohn, D. L., *The Good Old Days* (1940/1976)
Corfield, P. J., *Dress for Deference and Dissent* (Costume 23, 1989)
Cunnington, C. W., *Englishwomen's Costume in the 19th century* (1939); *Englishwomen's Costume in the Present Century* (1954)
Cunnington, C. W. and P., *Handbook of English Mediaeval Costume* (1953); *English Costume in the 16th Century* (1954); *English Costume in the 17th Century* (1955); *English Costume in the 18th Century* (1957); *English Costume in the 19th Century* (1968)
Daché, L., *Talking Through My Hats* (1946)
Davis, J., *Straw Plait* (1981)
De Marly, D., *Fashions for Men* (1985); *Louis XIV and Versailles* (1987)
Diderot, M., *Encyclopedie ou Dictionnaire Raisonne des Sciences des Arts et des Metiers, Le Chapelier* (1751-65)
Dony, J. A., *History of the Straw Hat Industry* (1936)
Doughty, R. W., *Feather Fashions and Bird Preservation* (1975)
Earle, A. M., *Two Centuries of Costume in America 1620-1820* (1903)
Eelking, H. M., *Lexicon der Herrenmode* (1960)

Encyclopedie Methodique des Sciences...Le Chapelier (1787)

Evans, J., *Dress in Medieval France* (1952)

Fairholt, F. W., *Costume in England* (1848)

Franklin, A., *La Vie Privée des Autrefois* (1903); *Dictionnaire Historique des Moeurs* (1905-6)

Freeman, C., *Luton and the Hat Industry* (1953)

Generall Description of All Trades (1747)

Ginsburg, M., *Victorian Dress in Photographs* (1980); *Paris Fashion* (1989)

Glassé, Cyril, *Concise Encyclopedia of Islam* (1989)

Gresham Publishing, *Modern Drapery and Allied Trades* (1912)

Hale, N. C., *Pelts and Palisades* (1959)

Harmand, J., *Jeanne D'Arc et ses costumes...* (1929)

Harrison, M., *The History of the Hat* (1960)

Haweis, M. E., *The Art of Dress* (1879)

Hawkins, J. H., *History of the Worshipful Company of the Art and Mystery of Feltmakers of London* (1917)

Howell, Mrs, *Handbook of Millinery* (1847)

Inder, P., *18th century Hats in Exeter Museum* (Costume 7, 1973)

Knight, C., *Cyclopoedia of the Industrial Arts* (1851); *Pictorial Gallery of the Arts* (1853)

Lady, *How to Dress of £15 pa* (1878)

Lady, *The Workwoman's Guide* (1836/1840)

Le Blanc, *Art in Ornament and Dress* (1877)

Levitt, S., *The Victorians Unbuttoned* (1985)

McClellan, M. E., *Felt Silk Straw Hand-made Hats, Tools and Processes in the Bucks County Historical Society* (Doyleston Pa 1977)

McCrumm, E., Ed, *David Shilling: the hats* (1981)

Melton, H., *Hints on Hats adapted to the Heads of the People* (1853)

Mendes, V. M., *Hats as Art* (V & A Album, Spring 1989)

McCulloch's Commercial Dictionary (1859)

Mintel, *Report on Hats and Scarves* (1988/89)

Montsarrat, A., *And the Bride Wore...* (1973)

Munich Stadtmuseum, *Von Kopf bis Hut* (1978)

Musée de la Mode et du Costume, Paris, *Chapeaux 1750-1960* (1980); *Indispensables Accessoires XV1-XXe siècle* (1984)

Nederlands Kostuummuseum, The Hague, *125 Hoeden* (1986)

Nevinson, J.L., Ed., *Mundus Muliebris or the Ladies Dressing Room Unlock'd: The Correct Dress of the Head* (Costume Society Extra Series, 2/5)

Nollet, J.A., *L'Art de faire des chapeaux* (1765)

Palmer White, J., *Poiret* (1976); *Schiaparelli* (1986)

Penny Encyclopedia (Vol 23, 1942)

Picken, M. Brookes, Miller, D.L., *Dressmakers in France* (1956)

Polan. B., *Hats 84* (The Fashion Year, 1983)

Postlethwayt, M. *A Dictionary of Trade and Commerce* (1757)

Probert, C., *Hats in Vogue since 1910* (1981)

Rendell, T.J., *Millinery Techniques in the 1920's* (Costume 12, 1978)

Repton, J. Adey, *Observations on the Various Fashions of Hats, Bonnets or Coverings for the Head* (Archaeologia XXIV 1832; XXVII 1838)

Ribeiro, A., *Dress in 18th Century Europe* (1985); *Fashion in the French Revolution* (1988)

Riley, H.T., Ed., *Memorials of London and London Life in the 13th, 14th, and 15th Centuries* (1868)

Robb and Anne Edwards, *The Queens Clothes* (1976)

Rothstein, W., Ed., *Four Hundred Years of Fashion at the Victoria and Albert Museum* (1986)

Rubens, A., *A History of Jewish Costume* (1976)

Sachs, H., Amman, J., *Book of Trades* (reprint 1973)

Sadler, A., *175 Years of Hats* (Christy and Sons, 1948)

Savary, J., *Dictionnaire de Commerce* (1745)

Schoeffler, O.E. & Gales, C., *Esquire Encyclopedia of Men's Fashions* (1973)

Sears Roebuck Catalog facsimiles (1897; 1902; 1908; 1927)

Sims, G.R., *Living London* (1902); *One Hundred Years After (Henry Heath hatters)* (1922)

Smith, D.M., *The Hatting Industry in Denton Lancs* (Industrial Archaeology 3 (1) 1966)

Smith, J.H., *The Felt Hat Industry 1500-1850* (Transactions of the Lancs and Cheshire Antiquarian Society 69, 1959); *The Hatters* (nd)

Taylor, L., *Mourning Dress* (1983)

Thaarup, A., *Heads and Tales* (1956)

Tmidior, *Der Hut* (1914)

Tomlinson's Encyclopedia of Useful Arts and Manufactures (1854)

Treue, W., *Das Hausbuch der Mendelschen Zwolfbruderstiftung* (1965)

Turin Exhibitions, Duboc H Groupe XX (1913)

UK Government, *Central Statistical Office Business Monitor Hats Caps and Millinery* (PQ 4537) (1988-9)

Unwin, G., *Industrial Organisation in the 16th and 17th centuries* (2nd ed, 1963)

Ure, A., *Dictionary of Arts* (1867)

Whitbourn, F., *Mr Lock of St. James's Street* (1971)

Wilcox, R.T., *The Mode in Hats* (1945); *5 Centuries of American Costume* (1963); *The Dictionary of Costume* (1970)

Wildblood, J., *The Polite World* (1957)

Willis, R., *A Book of London Yesterdays* (1960)

Wohl, A.S., *Endangered Lives: Public Health in Victorian Britain* (1983)

THESIS MATERIAL

Ginsburg, L., *Morale and Economy: The Government's Consumer Policy in World War II with particular reference to Women's Clothing* (Unpublished Thesis, History Department, University of York, UK, 1987)

Smith, J.H., *Development of the English Felt Hat and Silk Hat Trades 1800-1912* (Unpublished Thesis, University of Manchester, UK, 1980)

ARCHIVE MATERIAL

Fashion Institute of Technology, *Interviews with Alfred Solomon, Janet Sloane* (Special Collections TT 139.073 nV77; TT 139.073 V 76); University of Manchester, UK, John Rylands Library, *Diary of Dorothy Richardson 1779* (M/S 1125 pp206-207-208); University of Sussex, UK, Mass Observation Archive; Victoria and Albert Museum, Liberty Catalogs passim.

PERIOD REPRODUCTIONS of fulled and knitted caps 16th-19th century including both Flat and Monmouth caps may be obtained from Kirstie Buckland, Chippenham Gate, Monmouth, Gwent NP5, UK.

Index

Adams, Abigail, 61
Adrian, 117
Agnés, Mme., 115
Alexandra, Princess of Wales, 85, *91*
Alpine hat, 108, 126
Amies, Hardy, 133
Amman, Jost, *33*
Amuce, 23
Anatomie of Abuses; 34
Anderson, Don, *151*
Androsmane hat, l', *64*, 66
Animals, trimming with, 92
Anne of Bohemia, 27
Anne of Denmark, 44, *45*
Arnold, J., 43
Arnolfini Marriage, The, 23, 24
Arnt, Eric Moritz, 14

Art Goût Beauté, 114, 117
Art of the Feltmaker, The, 17
Ascot, 6, 137, 138, *140*
At the Milliners, 90
Austen, Jane, 78
Avril, Suzanne, *98*

Babushka, 123
Badge, hat as, 13, 14
Baker Boy berets, 129, *130*
Baldung, H., *37*
Balenciaga, Cristobal, 123, *123*, 128, *128*
Ball on Shipboard, A, 92
Ballard, Bettina, 123
Ballin, Ada S., 104
Banton, Travis, 116, 118
Barbier, George, *103*

Barrell, Cynthia, *127*
Basque beret, 117, 148
Beaton, Cecil, 7, *118*, 120, 122
Beau Brummel, 85
Beaver 6, 22, 23, 31-35, *32*, 44
  animal, 54
  export of, 45
Beefeaters, 32, *33*
Bellini, G. *11*
Benedict, Zadoc, 68
Berthault, P.G., *15*
Berthe, 93
Bertin, Rose, 14, *59*, 59-62
Billycock hat, 88
Bismarck, 15
Blanchot, Jane, *117*
Bloomer, Amelia, 83
Boaters, 87, 98, 127
Bochstensmannen Och Hans Drakt, 24
Boileau, Etienne, 19
Bollinger, 83, 88
Bon Genre, Le, 73, *74*
Bonnets, making, 78
Book of Trades, 33

Booth, Charles, 101
Borsellinos, 125
Bosse, Abraham, *46*
Bow, Clara, 116, *116*
Bowes, Sir Jeremy, *36*
Bowler hat, 87, 88, 107, 124, 125
Bowles, Carrington, *62*
Boy Scout hat, 87
Boyd, John, 148, 150
Breton Sailors, 133
Brewer, E. Cobham, 14
Brigade of Guards, The, 6
British Costume, The, 94
British Felt Hat Manufacturers, 8
Bronze Age
  caps, 18, *19*
  hairnets, *19*
Brown, Victoria, 147, *148*
Burdett, Peter Perez, *58*
Bury, Lady Charlotte, 73

Calache hood, *62*, 63
Cambridge hat, 88
Campbell, R., 56

Cap of Maintenance, 13
Caprice, Le, 94
Caps
  Bronze Age, 18, *19*
  cloth, 127
  English, *40*
  flat, *37,* 87, 88, 110
  house, 62, 63, 75, 77
  indoor, *93*
  informal, 39, 41
  knitted, 22, 36
  lace, *55,* 56
  Monmouth, 36, 37, 47
  Montero, 47, 88
  night, 37, 38
  patterns for, *79*
  pillbox, 83
  soft, 127
  sports, 110
  widow's, 84
Cardin, Pierre, 128, 129
Carroll, Lewis, 89
Carrying the Law in the Synagogue, 10
Celnart, Mme., 78
Cérémonies Religieuses du Monde, Les, 12
Chanel, Gabrielle, 101, 114
Chapeau Bras, 66
Chaperon, 23-25
Charles V of France, crowning, *14*
Charles VII of France, 17, 23
Christic and Sons, 148
Christy's, 108
City Match, 44
Claire, Ina, 118
Clegg, Andrew, 70
Cloche, 7, 114, *115*
Clothing trades, 19
Cocked hats, 85
Coffingnon, M., 100, 101
Coiffures et rubans à l'Italienne et
  coiffures grecques, 73
Colbert, Baptiste, 52
collapsible hats, 86, 87
Concise Encyclopedia of Islam, 11
Coronations, 12, 13
Coryate, Thomas, 58
Costumes Anglais et Français, 74
Cottage bonnet, 75, 81
Coulisses de la Mode, Les, 100
Counter's Commonwealth, The, 44
Courrèges, 7, 128, 129
Cowboy hats, 87
Cranach, Lucas the Elder, *34*
Crawford, M.D.C., 115
Croker, Mrs John, *42*
Croquet Players, *83*
Crosby, Bing, *126*
Crown of St. Edmund, 13
Crudities, 58
Crusher hats, 109
Cumberland hat, 85
Cunnington, Dr. C. Willett, 92
Curtis, Tony, 135

D'Attainville, Vladzio, 123
Daché, Lilly, 8, 9, 101, 118, 123
Damita, Lili, 120
Dan, George, 148
de Bourbon, Blanche, 23
de Bourbon, Jeanne, 24
de Bruyn, Abraham, *41*
de Critz, Paul *44, 45*
de Hoogh, R., *12*
de Maintenon, Marquise, 52
de Pisan, Christine, 27
de Saussure, Charles, 57
de Scorailles de Roussillhe, Marie Adelaide

51, 52
Debard, Christine, 6
Debard, Pierre, 6
Deerstalkers, 110
Defraine, *64*
Degas, Edgar, *90*
Delineator, The, 101
Demi castor, 45
Demokratenhut, 15
Denford, Carole, 146
Derby Day, 82
Derby, 88, 107, *108,* 125
Dietrich, Marlene, 118, 120
Dior, Christian, 127, *128*
Disco hat, 148
Doll hat, 122
Dolly Varden bonnets, 85
Dufourmantelle, Madame, *94*
Dunand, Jean, 115
Dunlap hat, 107

Eddy, Mrs. Augustus Newland, 100
Eden, Anthony, 109
Edward III, 23
Edward VII, *106,* 124
Edwards, Anne, 122
Eisenhower, General, 109
Elizabeth I, 43
Elizabeth II, 133, 134
Elizabeth Valois hat, 73
England, fur trade in, 32
English hood, 39
Eric, *119*
Esterel, Jacques, *131*
Eton, 6
Eugénie hat, 117
Evelyn, Mary, 52

Fanchon bonnets, *79, 82,* 83
Fanny, Mlle., 78
Fastolf, Sir John, 23, 24
Feathered half hat, 128
Feathers, 92, 94
Fedora, 108
Fellowes, Daisy, 118
Felt hats, 17-23, 66-71, *68, 69*
  making, *105*
Fenner, William, 44
Field Marks, 46
Figures à la Mode, 12
Firbank, Heather, 103
Fluegel, J.C., *9*
Fontange, 52, 53
Fouquet, Jean, *17*
Four Seasons, The, 48
'Four Stories and a Basement', 92
Fox, Freddie, 6, 7, 133, 139, *143*
Fox, George, 12
France, fur trade in, 31, 32
Franklin, Alfred, 22, 45
Franklin, Benjamin, 66
Frazier, Agnes, 77
Frazier, Brenda, 118
French hood, 38
French Revolution, hats in, 14
Frith, W.P., *82*

Gainsborough, Thomas, *58, 60,* 64
Galerie des Modes, 61
Garbo, Greta, 117
Garibaldi, Guiseppe, 15, 83
Gazette du Bon Ton, 113
Gentlemen hatters, 67
George V, crowning of, *13*
Gervex, Henry, *100*
Geywood, Richard, *48*
Gibus, Antoine, 87

Glassé, Cyril, 11
Godwin, E.A., 97
Godwyne, John, 21
Gower, George, 42
Grable, Betty, 118
Grace Before Meat, 49
Grands Chroniques de France, 17
Greenaway, Kate, 97
Grey, Lady Jane, *39*
Guérin, Mme., 78
Guy, Maria, 115, *117*
Gypsy bonnet, 72

Harrison, Michael, 25
Harrisson, Tom, 120
Harrow, 6
Hartnell, Norman, *121,* 133
Harvesters, The, 61
Hat Act, 68
Hat Conformer, *152*
Hat honor, 12
Hat, The, 10
Hat-making, 70, 71
Hatpins, 112
Hats
  badge, use as 13, 14
  early nineteenth century, 72-89
  eighteenth century, 55-71
  importance of, 8
  language, in, 16
  later nineteenth century, 90-112
  machine-made, 107
  military, 46
  respectability, sign of, 104
  seventeenth century, 44-54
  sixteenth century, 31-43
  status symbol, as, 12
  twentieth century, 113-138
Hatters Gazette Diary, 104
Hawes, Elizabeth, 123
Headdresses, 25-28, *26, 29, 30,* 51-53
Heads and Tails, 103, 120
Heath, W., 76
Hechter, Daniel, *130*
Helmet hats, 72
Henrietta Maria, *48*
Henry VIII, *33*
Herbault, Mme., 78
Hidatso dancer, *9*
High hats, 15
  making, 105-107
History of Jewish Costume, A, 11
History of Knitting, 36
History of the Hat, The, 25
Hofnaegel, Joris, *35*
Holbein, Hans, 32, *33, 38, 39*
Hollar, Wenceslaus, 48, *48, 49*
Homburgs, *107,* 108, 124, *126*
Homer, Winslow, *83*
Hoods, 23, 24
Hopkins, Everard, *97*
Horseman, Bill, 140, 147
Horsleydown Wedding, The, 35, 49
Hudibras Redivivus, 48
Hudson Bay Company, 45
Hulanicki, Barbara, 129
Hurers, 20
Hyde Park walking dress, *74*
Hystoire de Helayne, L', 28

J.B. Stetson hat, *106,* 109
James I, 44
Jardin de La Noblesse, Le, 46
Jelfs, Yvette, 140
Jews, 23, *24*
  heads, covering, 11
John of France, 24

John, Mr., 117, 118, 120
Jones, Stephen, 146, *147*
Journal des Modes, 103

Kangol, 148
Kennedy, Jackie, 133, *136*
Khevenhüller hat, 63, 64
Kitson, Lady, *42*
Knox hat, 107
Kossuth hats, 15, 87
Kossuth, Lajos, 15, 87

Lafayette, General, 66
Lamballe hats, 85
Lanvin, Jeanne, 101, *115*
Lauren, Ralph, *141*
Laver, J., *72*
Le Nain, *49*
Leloir, Heloise, *82*
Lens, Bernard, 55, *55*
Lepape, Georges, *102, 113*
Liberty's, 94, 97
Liedet, Loyset, *28*
Living London, 99
Livre des Mestiers, 19
Locke's of St. James, 87, 88
London hatters, 20
London Tradesman, The, 56
Lord and Lady Clapham dolls, *53*
Louis of Anjou, *25*
Lowenstein, Count of, *37*
Lucas, Otto, 7, 129
Lucile, *1-4,* 101, 103.
Lydgate, Dom, 25

Mad hatters, 69, 89
Madcaps, 101
Magasin des Familles, Le, 82
Mail order, 94, 95, 99
Maillard, M., *152*
Maison Michel, 6, 7
Marie Antoinette, 59
Martyrdom of St. Barbara, The, 21
Mary Countess Howe, *58*
Mary Queen of Scots, 39
Mass Observation, 120, 121, 123, 124
Mathieu, M., *45*
Medieval times, hats in, 17-30
Melnikoff, Ellen, 133
Memorials of Old London, 21, 22
Mercury, use of, 69, 89
Merry Widow hat, 103, *104*
Metcalfe, Betsy, 59, 80
Mignard, Paul, *51*
Miranda, Carmen, 118
Mirman, Simone, 6, 133, 134
Mob-caps, 114
Modernes Incroyables, Les, 74
Modes, Les, 72, *60,* 119
Monmouth cock, 50, 51
Monnier, Le, *117*
Montana, Claude, *142*
More, Sir Thomas, *38*
Moulthrop, R., *63*
Mourning, 84
Muir, Jean, 147
Mundus Muliebris, or The Ladies Dressing
  Room Unlock'd, 52
Munksgaard, E., 18
Muslims
  heads, covering, 11

Nain, Le, *49*
New Look, 127
Nightcaps, 37, 38
Nivernois hat, 64
Nockert, M., 24

Numa, 77

Oldtidsdragter, 18
Oliver, Frank, *151*
Oliver, Isaac, *36, 40*
Omnium Poene Europae, Asiae, Aphricae, Atque Americum Gentium Habitus, 41
One-eyed hat, 116

Pacquin à 5 heures, 100
Panama hats, 110
Panckoucke's *Encyclopédie, 68*
Pantheon Macaroni, The, *64*
Parry, John, 80
Patou, Jean, 114, 115
Paulette, Mme., 7
Peacock Revolution, 135
Penn, William, 12
Pepys, Samuel, 12, 44, 48, 50, 57
Perrit, Sally Sandford, *63*
Peter Robinson, 79
Petitpierre, A.C., 10
Pett, Phineas, *38*
Phrygian cap, 12, 14
Picard, B., *12*
Picture hat, 116
Pilgrim hats, 48
Pinpoints, 120
Pixie hood, 122
Poiret, Paul, 101, *102,* 103
Pokes, 73
Polan, Brenda, 144
Pork-pie hat, 125, 126
Presley, Elvis, 135
Princess Diana, 111, 148, *150*
Prussian students, hats of, 14
Psyche, 77
Psychology of Clothes, The, 9
Puff Ball Toques, 133

Quakers, 12, 64
Quant, Mary, 7, 129, 133
Queen Elizabeth the Queen Mother *119*, 120, 133
Queen Elizabeth's Wardrobe Unlocked, 43

Ramillies, cock, 51
Read, Benjamin, 76
Reapers, The, 61, *65*
Reboux, Caroline, 100, 115, 116, 118
Red Cap of Liberty, 14, *15,* 66
Religious ritual, baring or covering head in, 10-12
Review, The, 57
Richardson, Dorothy, 70
Richmond, Countess of, 39
Roberts, Robert, 104
Roman de la Rose, Le, 30
Roman hooded cloak, *18*
Roosevelt, Teddy, 15, 87
Rothstein, W., *10*
Round hats, 66
Rubens, Alfred, 11
Rudolph, *129*
Rutt, Richard, 36

Sandoz, Frederick, 97, *99*
Schiaparelli, Mme., 101, 117, 118, *118*
Sears, Roebuck, *95, 96,* 97, *99, 106, 116, 119*
Shelton, John, 34
Sherburne, Annie, 147
Shilling, David, 137, 146, *148*
Shilling, Gertrude, 137, 146
Shilton, Jane, 133
Shiraz, felt hat-making in, *22*
Shoe hat, 118
Shop catalogs, 94, 95
Shopping hat, 120
Shulkan Aruch, 11
Siddons, Sarah, 60
Silk hats, 107
Simms, J.R., 99
Simon, John, 89
Simpson, Mrs., 120
Sloane, Janet, 150
Slouch hats, 46
Smith, C.A., *80*
Smith, Graham, 6, 148, *151*
Smith, T.B., 80
Soft felts, 107, 109
Solomon, Alfred, 101, 118, 123

Somerset, Countess of, *40*
Somerville, Philip, 6, 133, *139, 144,* 147
Spartary, 101
Sports headgear, 126, 127
Spreiregen, Jacques, 148
St. Clement, 17
St. Igny, Jean, *46*
St. Jean, *52*
St. Paul, 10, 11
Statute of Apparel, 26, 37
Steen, Jan, *35, 49*
Steeples, 45
Stone, Benjamin, *107*
Straw hats, 57-59, *75,* 78, 81, 82, 97. 98, *108,* 109, 110, 127
making, *80, 81*
Straw splitters, *81*
Stubbes, Philip, 34, 42, 44
Stubbs, George, 61, *65*
Sugar Loaves, 45, *46*
Suzy, 122
Swanson, Gloria, 116
Sweden, opposing constitutional factions, 14

Talbot, Suzanne, 118
Talking Through My Hat, 8
Taste and Fashions, 72
Telescope hat, 126
Tell, William, 9, *9,* 10
Thaarup, Aage, 103, *119,* 120, 122
Thanet hat, 88
Thelma, Lady Furness, 120
Thomas, Ian, 133
Tissot, J., *92, 93*
Titfer, 16
Tomlinson, J., 17
Tonga, covering of heads in, 10
Top hats, 15, 72, 85, 88, 124
Toques, *92, 94*
Trachtenbuch, *51*
Traveling hats, 23, 92
Treacy, Philip, *152*
Très Riches Heures du Duc de Berry, 21
Trilby, 108
Truth of Our Times, The, 46

Tudor styles, 97

Vallée, H., *103*
Valois, Rose, 115
van der Donck, Adriaan, 31, 45
van Dyck, Anthony, *48*
van Ecyk, Jan, 23, *24*
Veils, 19
Venice, *11*
Vernet, Carle, 73, *74*
Vernier, Rose, 133
Victor, Sally, 118
Victoria, Queen, 84, *84,* 85
Victorine, Mme., 78
Vionnet, Madeleine, 116
Virot, Maison, 100
von Khevenhüller, Field-Marshal, 63
von Meteren, Herman, 41
Vrelant, Guillaume, 28

Waist and Extravagance, 75, 76
Wallace, Lucy, 101
Way of the World, The, 34
Wedding headdress, 111
Wedge, James, 129
Wedgwood Family, The, 65
Wellington hat, 85
Westwood, Vivienne, *146*
Wide-brimmed felts, 87
Wilson, Francis, 46, 47
Wok hat, 147, *148*
Wong, Anna May, 120
Woodward, Kirsten, *144*
Woolands, 103
Wooly hats, 46, 47
Workwoman's Guide, The, 79
Worsley, T. & J., 108
Worth, Charles, 83, 85, 99, 100
Wright, Joseph, *58*
Wright, W., 120, *139,* 148

Yeomen of the Guard, 32, *33*

Acknowledgments

To Cora Ginsburg of New York, who has helped me to appreciate fashion's past and to Alan Couldrige of the Royal College of Art, London, who has shown me that it has a future — and to Leslie and David.

Sincere thanks to the many who helped with this book and have with so much kindness and good humor provided advice, assistance and expertize:

Peter Ackroyd, Helen Alexander, Sir Hardy Amies, Pat Baker of Plymouth Plantation, Ian Bayley, Peter Brandon, Victoria Brown, Casey Bush, Millinery Institute, New York, Christy and Co., Fiona Clark, Jill Clements (British Hat Guild), Peter Cooke, Costume Institute, Metropolitan Museum of New York, Celestine Dars, Karin Finch, Freddie Fox, Gallery of English Costume, Manchester, Mr Garvin, Stockport Museum, Sarah Gibbings, Lucy Ginsburg, Bill Horseman, Yvette Jelfs, Mr John, Stephen Jones, Marylebone Reference Library (Westminster Public Libraries), Richard Martin of the Fashion Institute of Technology, Reina Marcusson, Simone Mirman, Museum of Costume and Fashion Research Centre, Bath, Museum of Mankind, Marion Nicholl of the Wardown Park Museum, Luton, Jo-An Olian of the Museum of the City of New York, Rupert Radcliffe-Genge, Royal College of Art, Annie Sherburne, David Shilling, Sears Roebuck, Graham Smith, Phillip Somerville, Kay Staniland of the Museum of London, Francoise Tétard Vittu, Philip Treacy, Victoria and Albert Museum, London, Jack Walworth, James Wedge, Wellcome Institute for the History of Medicine, Frank Whittemore, Major Wright, Kate Woodhead, Kirsten Woodward.

Hatmaking can be studied at the Wardown Park Museum, Luton Bedfordshire, UK, and the Stockport Museum and Art Gallery, Stockport, Lancs, UK. There are good collections of hats, basic and fashionable, at the museums listed in the acknowledgments above and those whose catalogs are mentioned in the Bibliography.